OREGON
Trails and Horse Camps

By Kim McCarrel

25 Horse Camps & Equestrian-Friendly Parks
68 Trails to Explore on Horseback
Over 800 Miles of Trails

Ponderosa Press
Bend, Oregon

ON THE COVER:
Riders enjoy the Pacific Crest Trail near Lost Lake, with Mt. Hood in the distance.

Published by:
Ponderosa Press
64495 Old Bend Redmond Hwy., Bend, OR 97701
www.oregonhorsetrails.com
Copyright 2009
ISBN 978-0-615-26894-1

All rights reserved. No part of the material protected by this copyright notice may be reproduced or utilized in any form or by any means, electronic or mechanical, including photocopying, recording, or by any informational storage and retrieval system without written permission from the copyright owner. Published in the United States of America.

I've spent most of my life riding horses. The rest I've just wasted.
Anonymous

Contents

Contents 4
    Horse Camp Map 10
    Horse Camping Checklists 13

Baker Beach/Coast Horse Trails 17
Siuslaw National Forest
    Getting to Baker Beach 18
    Baker Beach Campground 20
    Dry Lake Trailhead Camp 21
    Horse Creek Trailhead Camp 22
    C&M Stables 23
    Baker Beach 24
    Baker Beach Dunes 26
    Coast Horse Trails 28
    Lily Lake Loop .30

Big Meadows Horse Camp 33
Willamette National Forest
    Big Meadows Horse Camp 34
    Getting to Big Meadows 35
    Duffy Lake & Beyond 36
    Pika/Fir Lakes .38
    Turpentine Loop 40

Box Canyon Horse Camp 43
Willamette National Forest
    Box Canyon Horse Camp 44
    Getting to Box Canyon Horse Camp . . .45
    Grasshopper/Chucksney Loop 46
    Lakes Loop 47
    McBee/Crossing Way Loop 48

Collier Memorial State Park 53
Chiloquin, Oregon
    Getting to Collier State Park 54
    Collier State Park Horse Camp 56
    Happy Trails Cowboy Campground. . . .57
    Collier-Kimball Trail 58

Contents   5

Rimrock Overlook 60
Spring Creek Headwaters 62
Williamson River Trail 64

Elijah Bristow State Park 67
Eugene, Oregon
Elijah Bristow State Park 68
Getting to Elijah Bristow State Park. ...69
Elijah Bristow State Park Trails 70

Joe Graham & Clackamas Lake Horse Camps 75
Mt. Hood National Forest
Getting to Joe Graham/
Clackamas Lake 76
Joe Graham Horse Camp 78
Clackamas Lake Horse Camp 79
Little Crater Lake Loop 80
PCT South to Warm Springs River 82
Timothy Lake Loop 84

Kelsay Valley Horse Camp 87
Umpqua National Forest
Kelsay Valley Horse Camp 88
Getting to Kelsay Valley 89
Calamut Lake 90
Lemolo Lake 92
Maidu Lake 94
Tenas Peak Loop 96
Tenas/PCT/Maidu Loop 98
Windigo Pass 100
Windigo/PCT/Tenas Loop 102

L.L. (Stub) Stewart State Park 105
Vernonia, Oregon
Hares Canyon Horse Camp 106
Getting to Stub Stewart State Park 107
Banks-Vernonia State Trail 108
Hares Canyon/B-V Loop 110
Holli's/Bumping Knots Loop 112

Contents

Lost Lake Horse Camp 115
Mt. Hood National Forest
    Lost Lake Horse Camp 116
    Getting to Lost Lake 117
    Jones Creek Road 118
    Lost Lake Butte 120
    Pacific Crest Trail North 122
    Pacific Crest Trail South 124
    Walking Trails 126

Mildred Kanipe Memorial Park 129
Umpqua, Oregon
    Mildred Kanipe Memorial Park 130
    Getting to Kanipe Park 131
    Mildred Kanipe Park Trails 132

Milo McIver State Park 137
Estacada, Oregon
    Milo McIver State Park 138
    Getting to Milo McIver State Park 139
    Milo McIver State Park Trails 140

Molalla River Corridor 145
Molalla, Oregon
    Molalla River Corridor 146
    Getting to Molalla River Corridor 147
    Molalla River Trails 148

Mt. Pisgah (Buford Recreation Area) 155
Eugene, Oregon
    Mt. Pisgah/Buford Recreation Area . . .154
    Getting to Mt. Pisgah 155
    Mt. Pisgah Trails 156

Nehalem Bay State Park 163
Nehalem, Oregon
    Getting to Nehalem Bay State Park . . .164
    Nehalem Bay State Park Horse Camp .165
    Bayocean House 166
    Bayocean Peninsula 168
    Bob Straub State Park 170

Contents 7

    Nehalem Bay State Park 172
    Sand Lake 174

Northrup Creek Horse Camp 177
Clatsop State Forest
    Northrup Creek Horse Camp 178
    Getting to Northrup Creek 179
    Northrup Creek Loop 180

Reehers Camp 183
Tillamook State Forest
    Reehers Camp 184
    Getting to Reehers Camp 185
    Gales Creek Trail 186

Sam Brown Horse Camp 189
Siskiyou National Forest
    Sam Brown Horse Camp 190
    Getting to Sam Brown Horse Camp . . .191
    Briggs Creek Trail 192
    Dutchy Creek Trail 194
    Onion Way Trail 196
    Taylor Creek Trail 198

Santiam Horse Camp 201
Santiam State Forest
    Santiam Horse Camp 202
    Getting to Santiam Horse Camp 203
    Mad Creek Canyon Loop 204
    Turnidge Creek Loop 208

Sevenmile Horse Camp 211
Willamette National Forest
    Sevenmile Horse Camp 212
    Getting to Sevenmile Horse Camp 213
    Old Santiam Wagon Road East 214
    Old Santiam Wagon Road West 216

Silver Falls State Park 219
Salem, Oregon
> Howard Creek Horse Camp 220
> Getting to Silver Falls State Park 221
> Buck Mountain Loop 222
> Rackett Ridge/Perimeter Loop 224
> Shellburg Falls 226
> 214 Trail/Smith Creek Loop 228

South Steens Campground 231
Frenchglen, Oregon
> South Steens Campground 232
> Getting to South Steens 233
> Big Indian Trail 234
> Little Blitzen Trail 236
> Riddle Ranch .238

Sunrise Valley Ranch 241
Maury Mountains, Ochoco National Forest
> Sunrise Valley Ranch 242
> Getting to Sunrise Valley Ranch. 243
> Double Cabin Loop 244
> Ranch Loop 246
> Volcano Spring/Logan Butte Loop 248

Triangle Lake Horse Camp 251
Mt. Hood National Forest
> Triangle Lake Horse Camp 252
> Getting to Triangle Lake Horse Camp .253
> Jefferson Park .254
> Lodgepole Trail 256
> Pacific Crest Trail North 258
> Pacific Crest Trail South 260
> Russ Lake Loop 262

Tryon Creek State Park 265
Portland, Oregon
> Tryon Creek State Park 266
> Getting to Tryon Creek State Park 267
> Tryon Creek Trails 268

Willamette Mission State Park 273
Salem, Oregon
    Willamette Mission Horse Camp 274
    Getting to Willamette Mission 275
    Willamette Mission Trails 276

Acknowledgements

I want to thank the wonderful people who explored these beautiful trails with me: Lydia Hemsley, Whitney Rhetts, Debbie Withrow, Connie Thornton, Ray Thornton, Suzi Lewis, Teresa Healer, Carla Inman, Julie Johnston, Della Webb, Mona Steinberg, ZoAnne Farmen, Cindy Webb, Tina Carr, Karen Kohler, Paul Latiolais, Stacy Livermore, Tess Simendinger, Lois Eagleton, Midge McGinnis, Cassie Richard, Alex Richard, Dennis Waldron and his family, Nancy Ring, Nancy Bruce, Diane Gueck, Larry Fildes, Sue Fildes, Matt Fildes, Nancy Wolf, Von Foster, Chuck Harrold, and Leo Skinner.

Special thanks go to Debbie Withrow, Lydia Hemsley, Whitney Rhetts, ZoAnne Farmen, Sue Fildes, and Marcia Anderton for their editing and proofreading assistance.

This book could not have been written without the enthusiastic support of my wonderful husband, Steve.

And of course I can't forget to thank Jane and Tex, my amazing Tennessee Walker mares. They enabled me to explore thousands of miles of trails in this beautiful state, and have a fabulous time doing it.

                                          Kim McCarrel

10 Horse Camp Map

Oregon Horse Camps

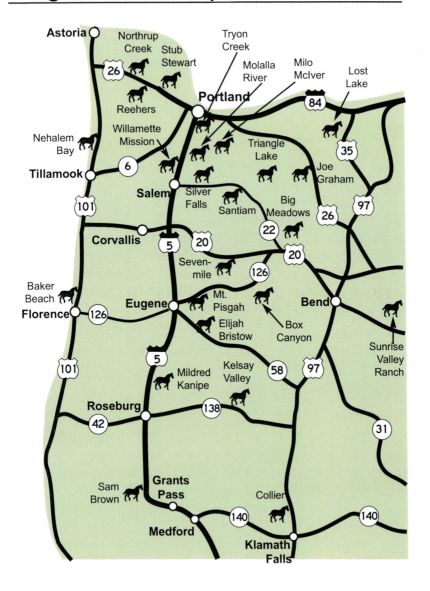

Horse Camp Map 11

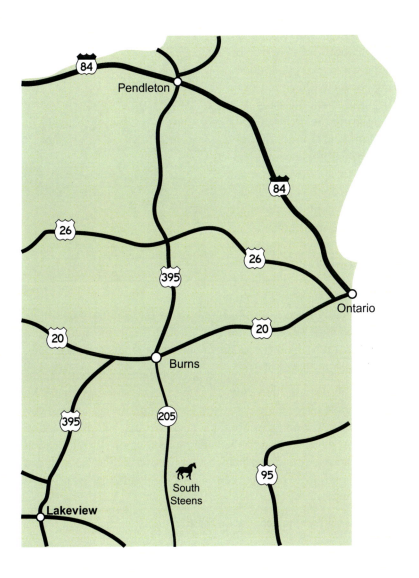

Foreword

Horse camping is a wonderful way to vacation. It's great to be out in the woods with your horse, sharing meals with your riding buddies and spending days at a time exploring the area trails. It can be time consuming, though, to research the horse camps you want to go to and then figure out where to ride once you get there. Some of our national and state forests provide useful data about their horse camps and trails, but others provide only sketchy information. And it's aggravating that forest maps don't tell you the things you really need to know, like how to find the trailhead from camp, what you'll see along the trail, how difficult the trail is, and whether or not it's suitable for a green horse or an inexperienced rider.

Photo: Jim Bordvedt

That's why this book was written--to provide equestrians with the information you need to plan your camping trip or your day ride. We hope this book encourages you to try out some horse camps you haven't been to yet and explore their nearby trails. The information provided here is as accurate as we can make it as of our publication date, but of course conditions change over time so we've also included information on how to contact each camp's local land manager for updated conditions.

Have fun, and I hope to see you on the trails!

Kim McCarrel

Horse Camping Checklist

Here's a list of things to pack for a horse camping adventure. Obviously, your own list will vary depending on the time of year and whether you are sleeping in a tent or in a camper or trailer. The list is fairly comprehensive, so it includes some things you probably won't need every time. (For instance, you probably won't need both a swimsuit and long johns on the same trip.) Hopefully this checklist will help you prepare for a wonderful trip.

Horse Equipment
saddle
girth
bridle
saddle pad
breast collar & crupper
halter & lead rope
equine first aid supplies
fly sheet
rain sheet
winter blanket
fly/mosquito spray
fly mask
hay or pellets
grain/supplements
hay bag or net
nose bag for feeding supplements
water buckets--2 or 3 (it's easier to carry water in 2 small buckets than one large one)
bungee cords to secure buckets
salt
brushes & curries
hoof pick
portable corral or high-line, tree savers, & carabiners if in area where no corrals are available
small tarp to keep hay dry
large tarp & ropes for rain cover/shade
stock water if none in camp
manure bucket
plastic garbage bags (some campgrounds use them)
manure fork
extra lead ropes
sponge
liniment

Camp Supplies
chair
camp table
firewood
matches and/or butane lighter
kindling
tarp (in case of rain)
camp stove
barbeque grill
propane
tablecloth
first aid kit
kleenex
extra batteries
checkbook (to pay camping fees)

Horse Camping Checklist (cont.)

Camp Kitchen
camp stove & fuel
coffee pot
cook pots
hot pads
can opener
spatula
tongs
plastic silverware
paper plates
paper cups
sharp knife
hand soap
toilet paper
sponge
aluminum foil
twine
paper towels
garbage bags
sandwich bags
basin for dishwashing
dishwashing liquid

Food
5+ gallons of potable water
breakfast supplies
lunch supplies
dinner supplies
snacks
beverages

Clothing
riding helmet
shirts
pants
boots
underwear
socks
pajamas
jacket or coat
sweaters or fleeces
warm hat
warm and/or waterproof gloves
clothes/shoes for in camp
swim suit
long johns
rain gear

Sleeping Equipment
sleeping bag or sheets/blankets
pillow
mirror
towel
washcloth
soap
toilet kit
suntan lotion
bug repellent
flashlight
any prescriptions you need

Trail Equipment
maps
GPS
compass
pocket knife
whistle
camera
saddlebags
first aid kit (see below)

survival kit (see below)
water bottles
hoof boot (in case of a lost shoe)

First Aid Kit for Saddlebags
6 Band-aids
2-inch Ace bandage
roll of vet wrap
triangular bandages
6 3-inch by 3-inch gauze pads
2-inch roller gauze bandage
5-10 years of adhesive tape
12 aspirin tablets
compress bandages with tails
small antiseptic agent
antiseptic ointment (betadine)
sunscreen
tweezers
equine thermometer
antihistamine cream for insect bites
any prescriptions you need
Banamine (available from your vet)

Trail Survival Kit
compass
GPS and extra batteries
maps for area you're riding in

cell phone
whistle on a cord
pencil & notebook
Leatherman-type tool with pliers, screwdriver, and knife
waterproof matches or butane lighter
9' x 12' emergency blanket
candle stubs for starting fires
30-gallon trash bag (for emergency poncho, ground cover, make-shift tent, and/or hauling water)
bouillon cubes (6+)
sugar cubes (6+)
tea bags (3+)
protein/energy bars
waterproof container
metal cup with a handle
shoelaces or dental floss and needle for tack repairs
wire pocket saw
flashlight or headlamp
extra batteries
metal mirror for signaling
hoof pick
pencil & notebook
light gloves
knit cap
jacket
rain gear
extra sox
toilet paper
duct tape
20 feet of cord
2 feet of wire
extra Chicago screws
hand/toe warmers
collapsible bucket

God forbid that I should go to any heaven in which there are no horses.

    R.B. Cunninghame-Graham,
       in a letter to President Theodore Roosevelt

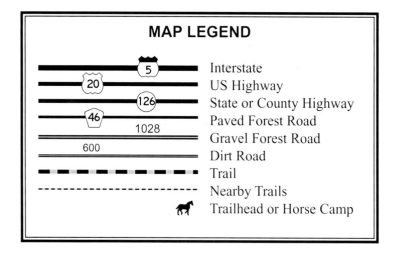

Baker Beach/ Coast Horse Trails

Siuslaw National Forest

Located just 1.5 hours from Eugene, Baker Beach provides access to the northern end of the spectacular Oregon Dunes. The Dunes run for 40 miles and are the longest stretch of coastal sand dunes in North America. You can ride beside the pounding surf, explore the dunes themselves, and observe the diverse animal and plant life that thrives in this unique ecosystem.

In addition to the wonderful beach riding in the area, there is an extensive network of mountain trails nearby. The Coast Horse Trails area offers lovely ocean vistas and interesting riding through coastal forest.

A late afternoon ride along Baker Beach.

Getting to Baker Beach

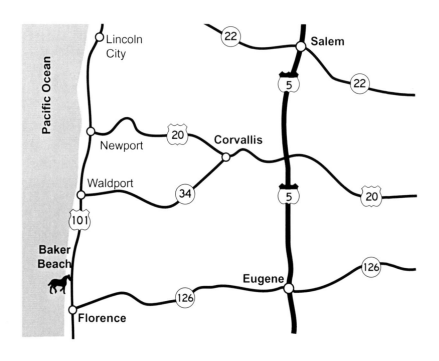

Baker Beach Area Trails

Trail	Difficulty	Elevation	Round Trip
Baker Beach	Easy	Sea Level	Varies
Baker Beach Dunes	Easy	Sea Level	8 miles
Coast Horse Trails	Moderate	500-1,500 ft.	Varies
Lily Lake Loop	Easy	Sea Level	1.8 miles

Baker Beach Area Horse Camps

Campground	# Sites	Elevation	Water	Reserv.
Baker Beach	5	Sea Level	None	No
Dry Lake Trailhead	2	1,100 ft.	Stock water	No
Horse Creek Trailhead	11	1,300 ft.	Stock water	No

Carla on Lexi, enjoying a stroll on the beach.

Baker Beach Campground

Directions: Located 60 miles west of Eugene, near Florence. From Florence, drive north on Highway 101 for 8 miles and turn left on Baker Beach Road (2 miles south of Sea Lion Caves). Continue 0.5 mile to the campground.

Elevation: Sea level

Campsites: 5 campsites. No corrals, but you can high-line your horses or bring portable corrals.

Facilities: Toilet. Parking for several trailers in the day-use area. No water.

Permits: User fee for campground. Northwest Forest Pass required for day-use parking.

Season: Year-round

Contact: Siuslaw National Forest, www.fs.fed.us/r6/siuslaw/, 541-902-8526

Debbie, Lydia, Tess, and Carla enjoy a sunny day at Baker Beach. Sea Lion Point is in the background.

Dry Lake Trailhead Camp

Directions: Located 60 miles west of Eugene, near Florence. From Florence, drive north on Highway 101 for 8 miles. Turn right on Herman Cape Road and follow it 2.5 miles to the trailhead.
Elevation: 1,100 feet
Campsites: 2 campsites with log corrals
Facilities: Toilet. Parking for several trailers in the day-use area. No water in camp, but stock water is available a short distance away.
Permits: None
Season: Year-round
Contact: Siuslaw National Forest, www.fs.fed.us/r6/siuslaw/, 541-902-8526

Teresa, Whitney, Lydia, and Tess reach the summit of Cape Mountain, not far from Dry Lake trailhead.

Horse Creek Trailhead Camp

Directions: Located 60 miles west of Eugene, near Florence. From Florence, drive north on Highway 101 for 8 miles. Turn right on Herman Cape Road and follow it 3.7 miles to the junction with Road 58. (You will pass Dry Lake trailhead after 2.5 miles.) Turn left and continue 1.3 miles to the trailhead. Or, drive 10.5 miles north of Florence on Highway 101, turn right on Horse Creek Road (Road 58), and continue 2.7 miles to the trailhead.

Elevation: 1,300 feet

Campsites: This trailhead has 11 campsites with 2-, 3-, or 4-horse log corrals.

Facilities: Toilet. Parking for 1 trailer per campsite. Parking for several additional trailers at the adjacent day-use area. There is no water at the camp, but stock water is available at a spring-fed trough a short distance away.

Permits: None

Season: Year-round

Contact: Siuslaw National Forest, www.fs.fed.us/r6/siuslaw/, 541-902-8526

Mist swirls among the trees at Horse Creek trailhead.

Debbie on Mel and Lydia on Shadow, riding on the beach just before sunset.

C & M Stables

If you are interested in boarding your horse while in the Florence area, C & M Stables offers reasonably-priced boarding facilities. Located at 90241 Highway 101, Florence, OR 97439, the stable is within easy riding distance of Baker Beach and a short drive from the Coast Horse Trails. Go to www.oregonhorsebackriding.com or call 541-317-0135 for reservations.

24 Baker Beach Area Camps

Baker Beach

Trailhead: Start at Baker Beach campground
Length: 7 miles round trip from the north end of the beach to Sutton Creek. 10 miles round trip from the trailhead to the Suislaw River.
Elevation: Sea level, of course
Difficulty: Easy
Season: Year-round
Permits: Northwest Forest Pass required
Facilities: Toilet. Parking for several trailers in the day-use area. No stock water is available.

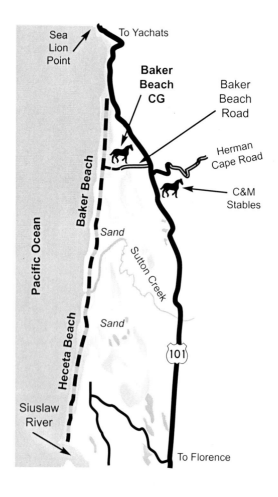

Tess on Dancer, Debbie on Mel, and Lydia on Shadow, enjoying a beautiful day at Baker Beach.

Highlights: It's hard to beat the exhilaration of riding your horse on Baker Beach. The waves crash on one side, the dunes roll into the distance on the other, and the sand stretches in front of you for miles. There are no houses or hotels along Baker Beach, which runs for 3 miles along the dunes. This beach is not heavily used, so you can safely canter your horse beside the waves. What a thrill!

The Ride: Take the short 0.3 mile trail from the parking area to the beach, and from there you can ride north 1.2 miles toward Sea Lion Point, or south 2 miles to Sutton Creek, which divides Baker Beach from Heceta Beach. If desired, you can cross Sutton Creek and continue riding on Heceta Beach another 2.7 miles to the Siuslaw River. Heceta Beach is fairly heavily used by people, so if your horse isn't comfortable with walkers, joggers, picnickers, dogs, whale watchers, or kite-flyers, it may be best to turn back at the Sutton Creek inlet that marks the end of Baker Beach.

26 Baker Beach Area Camps

Baker Beach Dunes

Trailhead: Start at Baker Beach Campground
Length: Up to 8 miles round trip. Several possible loops.
Elevation: Sea level
Difficulty: Easy
Season: Year-round
Permits: Northwest Forest Pass required
Facilities: Toilet. Parking for several trailers in the day-use area. No stock water is available.

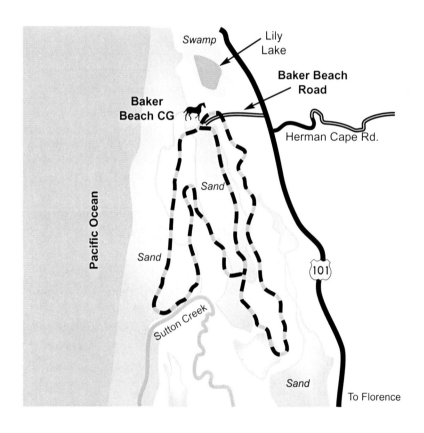

Carla on Lexi, Debbie on Mel, and Lydia on Shadow, riding along the dunes near Baker Beach.

Highlights: The Oregon Dunes are the largest coastal dune system in North America. The area trails give you a close-up view of this special ecosystem by providing several possible loops along the dunes and through the coastal vegetation near Baker Beach. The Snowy Plover, an endangered sparrow-sized shore bird, nests in the dry sand along the shore from May to September, so during this time be sure to stick to the trails and observe any signs that prohibit entry due to the presence of nesting Snowy Plovers.

The Ride: The trail departs from the Baker Beach campground. You can create several good loop rides along the dunes and through the dense stands of conifers that lie between the shifting sands. Because the dunes are dry and the sand is loose, in places your horse will be working in pretty deep footing.

28 Baker Beach Area Camps

Coast Horse Trails

Trailhead: Start at either Horse Creek Trailhead or Dry Lake Trailhead (see directions on pages 21-22)

Length: 50-mile network of trails. A number of loop rides of varying lengths are possible.

Elevation: 500 to 1,500 feet

Difficulty: Moderate -- trails traverse several steep hillsides and may be slippery after rain

Season: Year-round

Permits: None

Facilities: Toilet. Parking for many trailers. Stock water is available on the trail.

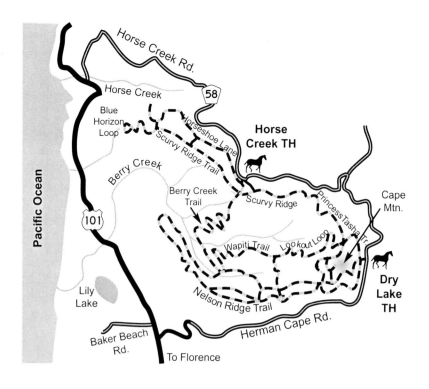

Highlights: The Coast Horse Trail system is a network of interconnected trails on the side of Cape Mountain, just north of Florence. The trails go along the crests of high ridges, follow switchbacks up and down steep mountain slopes, traverse old clear-cut areas, and meander through lovely old-growth forest. There is even a reconstructed 1915-era Indian hunting dwelling -- complete with an explanatory sign -- along the side of the trail. You can create your own loops to make your ride as long or as short as you like. The trail junctions have signs with maps of the trail system, so it's tough to get lost on these trails. There are nice views of the ocean from the summit of Cape Mountain and several other vantage points.

The Ride: All of the trails in this network are clearly marked. There are several springs for watering your horse and a couple of water crossings. In places the trail traverses steep hillsides, and while the heavy undergrowth will prevent most people from getting vertigo, appropriate caution should be taken. The trails can also become muddy and slick after a heavy rain.

Debbie and Mel take a breather on the Berry Creek Trail.

30 Baker Beach Area Camps

Lily Lake Loop

Trailhead: Start at Baker Beach Campground
Length: 1.8 miles round trip; several loops possible
Elevation: Sea level
Difficulty: Easy
Season: Year-round
Permits: Northwest Forest Pass required
Facilities: Toilet. Parking for several trailers in the day-use area at Baker Beach trailhead. No stock water is available.

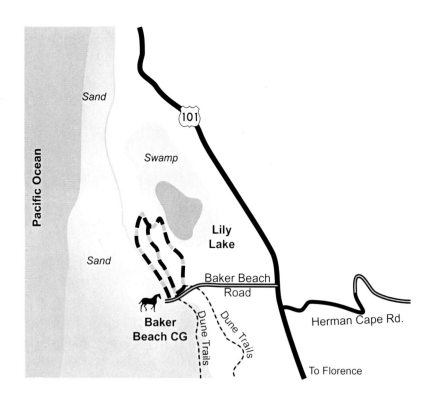

Highlights: This is actually 2 short, easy loops that wind through coastal vegetation, along the dunes, and beside the shore of Lily Lake. You can use these loops for a quick warm-up ride, or link them with segments of the dune trails to create a longer ride.

The Ride: The trail leaves from the eastern edge of the Baker Beach campground and winds through thick coastal vegetation beside Lily Lake and back along the dunes. There is no access to the lake because its banks are quite marshy.

Debbie on Mel, Carla on Lexi, and Lydia on Shadow, riding along the dunes near Lily Lake.

A man on a horse is spiritually as well as physically bigger than a man on foot.

John Steinbeck, The Red Pony

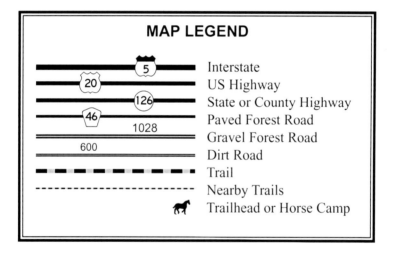

Big Meadows Horse Camp

Willamette National Forest

Located just off Highway 22 about 80 miles southeast of Salem, Big Meadows Horse Camp provides easy access to the western side of the Mt. Jefferson Wilderness. The beautiful North Santiam River runs through the area, which is dotted with numerous small and mid-size lakes. The trails are not difficult, and have only moderate elevation gain/loss. Wildflowers are plentiful and varied, even late in the summer. Bring your mosquito repellent, especially in late spring.

Some areas near the trails were badly burned in the 2003 B&B Fire, so while you may see more dead trees than you would like, you'll also have better mountain views than you would have a few years ago.

If the horse camp is full, you can find good primitive camping sites down Road 2257 near the North Santiam River. Day parking is available at both the horse camp and at nearby Duffy Trailhead.

Duffy Lake, near Big Meadows Horse Camp.

Big Meadows Horse Camp

Directions: Located about 80 miles southeast of Salem, 55 miles northwest of Bend, and 90 miles northeast of Eugene, off Highway 22. Turn east on Big Meadows Road (Road 2267) between mile posts 75 and 76. Continue 1 mile, turn left on Road 2257, and drive 0.5 mile to the horse camp. The road is paved all the way to the horse camp.

Elevation: 3,600 feet

Campsites: 9 campsites with 4-horse log corrals

Facilities: Toilets, potable water. Parking for 1 trailer per campsite. There is also a day-use parking area.

Permits: User fee for camping, or Northwest Forest Pass required for day-use parking

Season: May - October

Contact: Detroit Ranger District, www.fs.fed.us/r6/willamette/recreation/tripplanning/ index.html, 503-854-3366

Lydia and Teresa pump a bucket of water at Big Meadows.

Getting to Big Meadows

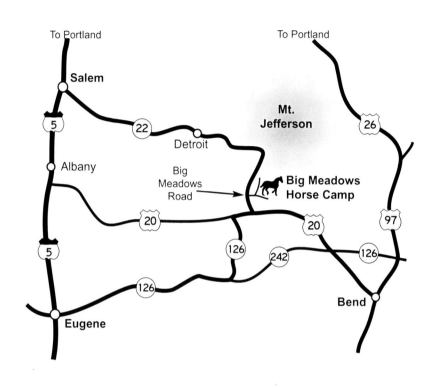

Big Meadows Area Trails

Trail	Difficulty	Elevation	Round Trip
Duffy Lake	Moderate	3,600-4,800	11 miles
Mowich Lake	Moderate	3,600-5,100	14 miles
Santiam Lake	Moderate	3,600-5,100	14 miles
Eight Lakes Basin	Moderate	3,600-5,200	18+ miles
Pika/Fir Lakes	Moderate	3,600-4,000	6 miles
Turpentine Loop	Challenging	3,600-4,600	15 miles

Duffy Lake and Beyond

Trailhead: Start at Big Meadows Horse Camp
Length: 11.3 miles round trip to Duffy Lake, 13.8 miles round trip to Santiam Lake, 14 miles round trip to Mowich Lake, or 18+ miles round trip to Eight Lakes Basin
Elevation: 3,600 to 4,800 feet for Duffy Lake, 5,125 feet for Santiam Lake, 5,090 for Mowich Lake, or 5,075 for Eight Lakes Basin
Difficulty: Moderate
Season: Summer through fall
Permits: User fee for horse camp, or Northwest Forest Pass required to park in day use area
Facilities: Toilet and potable water at the horse camp. Stock water is available on the trail.

Highlights: While this trail is rocky in places, the terrain is pretty, with old-growth forest along the way and Duffy Lake nestled against the base of Duffy Butte. In early July the blooming bear grass is beau-

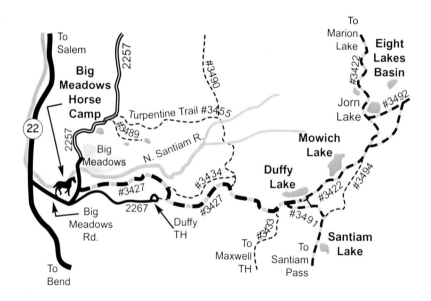

Bear grass blooming on the shore of Duffy Lake.

tiful. You can continue on the same trail to Mowich Lake and the Eight Lakes Basin beyond. Or you can turn right at the junction near Duffy Lake to reach Santiam Lake, which offers great views of Three Fingered Jack.

The Ride: The trail departs from the east edge of Big Meadows Horse Camp. The trail moves steadily uphill all the way to Duffy Lake, with several trail junctions along the way. Two miles from the horse camp, trail #3434 goes off to the left. Shortly afterward, the trail to the Duffy trailhead branches off to the right, and 1.3 miles beyond that, a connector trail to the Turpentine Trail goes to the left. After another 1.5 miles the trail to the Maxwell trailhead departs to the right. When you reach Duffy Lake, the trail continues toward Mowich Lake and the Eight Lakes Basin, or veers right to go to Santiam Lake and Santiam Pass.

If you want to continue on, Mowich Lake is 1.4 miles beyond Duffy Lake, and Santiam Lake is an additional 1.3 miles. Jorn Lake and the Eight Lakes Basin are 2 miles beyond Mowich Lake. You can see the upper slopes of Mt. Jefferson from several vantage points in the Eight Lakes Basin.

Big Meadows Horse Camp

Pika/Fir Lakes

Trailhead: Start at Big Meadows Horse Camp
Length: 5 miles round trip to Pika Lake
6 miles round trip to Fir Lake
Elevation: 3,600 to 4,000 feet
Difficulty: Moderate
Season: Summer through fall
Permits: User fee for horse camp, or Northwest Forest Pass required to park in day use area
Facilities: Toilet and potable water at the horse camp. Stock water is available on the trail.

Highlights: This is an easy, almost-level ride along a lightly-traveled gravel road and then on a well-maintained trail that leads through dense woods to Fir and Pika Lakes. It makes a good warm-up ride for your first day in camp, or a low-intensity ride on a day after you've tackled one of the more strenuous trails in the area.

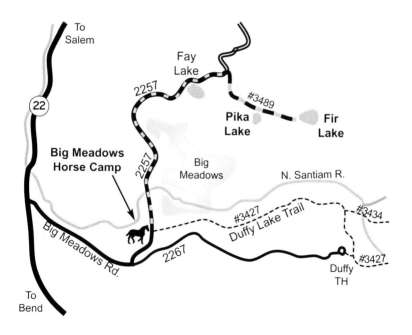

The Ride: Ride east out of Big Meadow Horse Camp and turn left on Road 2257. Follow it 1.6 miles to the very pretty Fay Lake, then continue another 0.4 mile and turn right on the well-marked trail #3489 to Pika Lake and Fir Lake. From here the trail winds through ancient woods about 0.5 mile to Pika Lake and then 0.5 mile farther to dead-end at Fir Lake. There is a nice picnic spot at Fir Lake.

The lovely Fir Lake.

Lydia on Shadow, Whitney on Cody, and Teresa on Radar, cooling off in the dense shade near Pika Lake.

Turpentine Loop

Trailhead:	Start at Big Meadows Horse Camp
Length:	15 miles round trip
Elevation:	3,600 to 4,600 feet
Difficulty:	Challenging: long, rocky trail, some steep slopes
Season:	Summer through fall
Permits:	User fee for horse camp, or Northwest Forest Pass required to park in day use area
Facilities:	Toilet and potable water at the horse camp. Stock water is available on the trail.

Highlights: This trail travels through dense forest, through areas ravaged by the B&B fire in 2003, and through meadows brimming with wildflowers. It then loops back along the North Santiam River and eventually joins the Duffy Lake trail for the return to the horse camp.

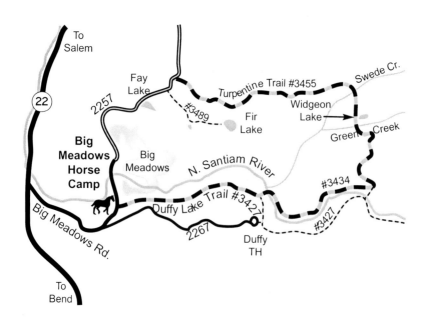

While the trail is long and in a few places it traverses steep hillsides, it's definitely worth the trek.

The Ride: Ride east out of Big Meadow Horse Camp and turn left on Road 2257. Follow it 2.1 miles (just past the turnoff for the Pika and Fir Lakes Trail #3489) and turn right onto the Turpentine Trail #3455. The trail is a dirt road at first, climbing steadily. Then just before the road ends, the trail veers off to the left. About 3 miles from the start of the Turpentine Trail you'll cross Swede Creek, pass Widgeon Lake, and cross Green Creek. There are several large meadows in this area that feature abundant wildflowers in season. Some sections of the trail were badly burned in the B&B fire. About a mile past Green Creek, a spur trail leading to the Duffy Lake Trail #3427 goes off to the left. Stay to the right. The trail runs along the bank of the North Santiam River for about 1.5 miles, then crosses the river and shortly afterward intersects with trail #3427. Veer right to return to Big Meadows.

Lydia and Shadow ride through a profusion of wildflowers in a meadow near Swede Creek.

No one can teach riding so well as a horse.

C.S. Lewis

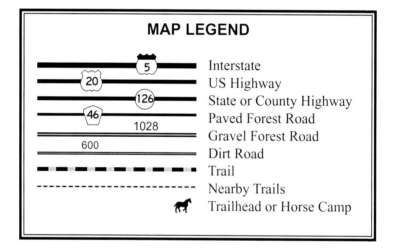

Box Canyon Horse Camp

Willamette National Forest

Box Canyon Horse Camp, on the western slope of the Cascades east of Eugene, was built in 1933 by the Civilian Conservation Corp. Two loop trails begin at the campground, and a short drive will take you to another loop trail that visits several lakes. A number of forest roads in the area provide additional riding opportunities.

Box Canyon is located in the deep canyon created by the South Fork of the McKenzie River, so some of the rides from camp involve significant elevation gain. While the trails themselves are not generally steep, there are places where the trails traverse steep hillsides. The Three Sisters Wilderness is on the east side of the canyon, the Waldo Lake Wilderness is on the south, and Chucksney Mountain Roadless Area lies to the west. The area is heavily forested so shade is plentiful, and wild rhododendrons and bear grass bloom profusely in season.

Wild rhododendrons grace the trail near Box Canyon Horse Camp.

Box Canyon Horse Camp

Directions: 80 miles east of Eugene and 100 miles west of Bend, off Highway 126. On Highway 126 between the towns of Blue River and McKenzie Bridge, turn south on Aufderheide Road (Forest Road 19) between mile posts 45 and 46. Continue 28 miles and turn right into the camp.

Elevation: 3,750 feet

Campsites: 11 campsites with 2-horse log corrals. Two of the sites are oversized and have 4-horse corrals.

Facilities: Toilets, stock water (which wasn't working when we were there in 2006 but has since been repaired), fire pits, picnic tables. Day parking is available for 2-3 trailers. No potable water.

Permits: None, no fee

Season: Summer through fall

Comments: Many of the campsites are surrounded by thickets of wild rhododendrons. When they are blooming in early July, they are a wonderful sight to wake up to.

Contact: McKenzie River Ranger District, www.fs.fed.us/r6/willamette/recreation/tripplanning/index.html, 541-822-3381

Tex and Jane relax at Box Canyon Horse Camp.

Getting to Box Canyon Horse Camp

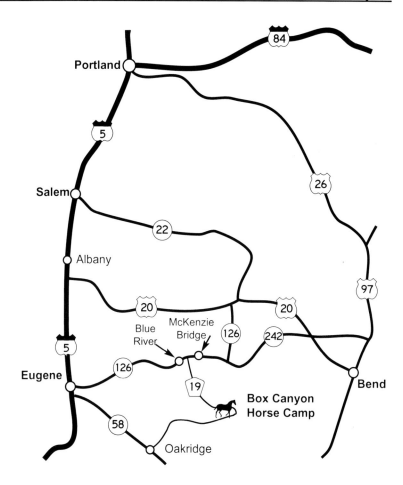

Box Canyon Area Trails

Trail	Difficulty	Elevation	Round Trip
Grasshopper/Chucksney	Challenging	3,750-5,700	10 miles
Lakes Loop	Moderate	4,550-5,100	8.5 miles
McBee/Crossing Way	Challenging	3,750-4,900	11 miles

Grasshopper/Chucksney Loop

Trailhead: The trail departs from Box Canyon Horse Camp
Length: 10 miles round trip
Elevation: 3,750 to 5,700 feet
Difficulty: Challenging--steep traverses, fallen trees
Season: Summer through fall
Permits: None
Facilities: Toilet. Parking for several trailers in the day-use area. Stock water is available at the horse camp, but there is no water on the trail.

Highlights: This trail provides beautiful forest riding as it winds past the top of Chucksney Mountain. In many spots the trail traverses very steep hillsides. Downed trees across the trail can be a problem, so call

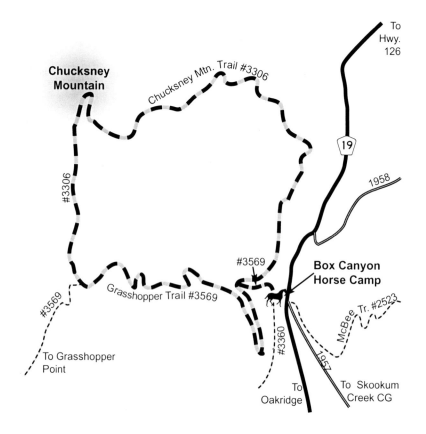

Connie and Lydia make their way up the Grasshopper trail.

the McKenzie Ranger District (541-822-3381) to determine whether the trails have been cleared.

The Ride: Pick up the Grasshopper Trail #3569 on the northwest side of the horse camp and follow it 0.25 mile to a fork that goes right to Chucksney Mountain or left to Grasshopper Ridge. If you want to take the steeper climb going out and the (somewhat) gentler slope coming back, stay to the left on the Grasshopper Trail. It climbs steadily, gaining nearly 2,000 feet of elevation in 3 miles. There are a few steep spots and a number of places where the trail traverses steep slopes. After 3.75 miles you'll reach a junction that goes left to Grasshopper Point in 5.5 miles or right to Chucksney Mountain on trail #3306. Go right, and in 2 miles you'll pass very near the summit of Chucksney Mountain (elev. 5,760 feet). From there the trail winds 4 miles back down to the horse camp, again traversing several very steep hillsides. This is a very good ride if the trails are cleared, and it reportedly offers great views of the Three Sisters from Chucksney Mountain. But when we were there in July 2006, there were numerous downed trees on the trails and we found it impossible to complete the loop (though not for lack of trying!).

Lakes Loop

Trailhead:	Start at Skookum Creek Campground, an easy 3.6 mile drive from Box Canyon Horse Camp. Drive out of the horse camp, turn right on Road 19 and almost immediately veer left on Road 1957. Continue 3.6 miles to Skookum Creek campground.
Length:	8.5 miles round trip
Elevation:	4,550 to 5,100 feet
Difficulty:	Moderate -- many water crossings
Season:	Summer through fall
Permits:	Northwest Forest Pass required to park at Skookum Creek trailhead
Facilities:	The campground has toilets and potable water. Stock water is also available on the trail. Plenty of parking for many trailers.

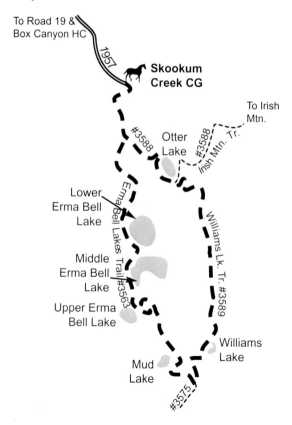

*Connie on Diamond and Lydia on Shadow,
soaking up the sun at Otter Lake.*

Highlights: This fun, forested trail takes you past several pretty lakes and across several streams. Bring plenty of mosquito repellent, because the bugs can be plentiful, especially early in the season.

The Ride: Pick up the trail at the entrance to the campground and follow it across the bridge over Skookum Creek. In 0.6 miles the trail forks, heading left toward Irish Mountain (trail #3588) and right to the Erma Bell lakes (named for a long-time forest service employee from the 1950's). Go to the left on the Irish Mountain Trail. You'll be returning via the Erma Bell Lakes Trail. After 0.5 mile you'll reach Otter Lake, which is dotted with lily pads. 0.3 miles farther you'll come to another trail junction. Trail #3588 to Irish Mountain continues to the left, but you will veer right on the Williams Lake Trail #3589 and in another 2.2 miles you'll reach Williams Lake. Continue 0.6 mile past Williams Lake and turn right at the trail junction toward the Erma Bell Lakes. Upper Erma Bell Lake is on the left in 0.4 miles, and 0.5 mile beyond is Middle Erma Bell Lake on the right. Continuing another 0.5 mile you'll pass Lower Erma Bell Lake, and on the way you'll hear the roaring of the falls as the creek that connects the lakes drops 200 feet in 0.1 mile. Continue on the Erma Bell Lake Trail to return to the trailhead.

McBee/Crossing Way Loop

Trailhead:	The trail departs from Box Canyon Horse Camp
Length:	11 miles round trip
Elevation:	3,750 to 4,900 feet
Difficulty:	The first half is challenging, as the trail is rocky and climbs steeply in places. The second half is easy.
Season:	Summer through fall
Permits:	None
Facilities:	The campground has toilets, stock water, and some day-use parking. No water is available on the trail.

Highlights: The first 8 miles of the ride are on single-track trails through a lovely mixed-conifer forest, with occasional views of distant ridges. The last leg of the ride is down a well-maintained forest road. In season, the blooming rhododendrons are amazing.

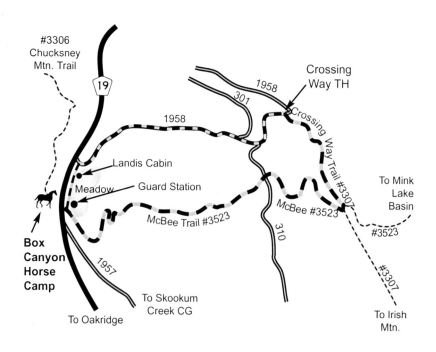

The Ride: From Box Canyon Horse Camp, cross Road 19 to the Box Canyon Guard Station and pick up the McBee Trail #3523 on the south side of the guard station. The trail climbs steadily and enters the Three Sisters Wilderness. After 3.6 miles it crosses Road 310, and 1.4 miles farther it intersects with the Crossing Way Trail. If you continue straight ahead on the McBee Trail, you'll eventually reach the Mink Lakes basin on the east side of the Cascades. If you turn right on the Crossing Way Trail #3307, you can go to Irish Mountain and the Pacific Crest Trail. Instead, turn left on the Crossing Way Trail, which slopes gently down for 1.9 miles to the Crossing Way trailhead. Turn left on Road 1958 and follow it downhill for 3.3 miles. Just before you reach Road 19 you'll cross McBee Creek as it runs through a lovely meadow. Turn left into the meadow (there is no trail here) and ride parallel to Road 19, past Landis Cabin to the Box Canyon Guard Station and the horse camp.

Teresa on Jane, admiring the blooming rhodies on the Crossing Way trail.

Some of my best leading men have been dogs and horses.

Elizabeth Taylor

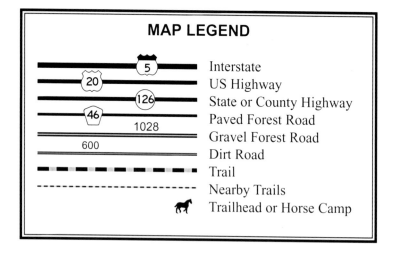

Collier Memorial State Park

Winema National Forest

Collier State Park is a beautiful spot a half hour north of Klamath Falls, near the town of Chiloquin. You can either camp in the park's semi-primitive campground (it has potable water, but the toilet is in the nearby day-use area) or at Happy Trails Cowboy Campground just across Hwy. 97. Both locations offer access to trails in the state park, beside the Williamson River, and in the Winema National Forest. Nearby attractions include world-class fly fishing on the Williamson River, food and fun at the Kla-Mo-Ya Casino, and a chance to see old-time logging operations at the Collier Logging Museum. But for equestrians, the real attraction is the variety in the area trails. Whether you enjoy riding along the river, through the forest, or along the rimrock, this area has wonderful trails to offer.

The lovely Williamson River runs through Collier Park.

Getting to Collier State Park

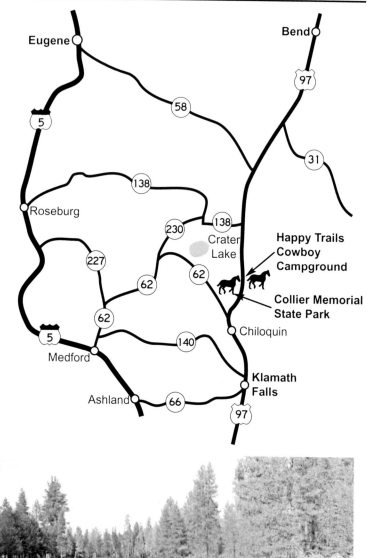

Beautiful Spring Creek flows near the horse camp at Collier Park.

Collier Area Horse Camps

Campgrounds	# Sites	Elevation	Water	Reserv.
Collier State Park	1	4,200	Yes	No
Happy Trails Cowboy Campground	15	4,200	Yes	No

Shadow and Tex hang out in the corrals at Collier Memorial State Park.

Collier Area Trails

Trail	Difficulty	Elevation	Round Trip
Collier-Kimball Trail	Easy	4,200-4,600	20 miles
Rimrock Overlook	Moderate	4,200-4,600	14 miles
Spring Cr. Headwaters	Easy	4,200-4,250	7.5 miles
Williamson River Trail	Easy	4,200	Varies

… Collier State Park

Collier State Park Horse Camp

Directions: 30 miles north of Klamath Falls or 100 miles south of Bend on Highway 97, between mileposts 243 and 244. Turn west off Highway 97 into Collier State Park, drive past the logging museum, and follow the signs 0.5 mile to the horse camp.

Elevation: 4,200 feet

Campsites: One semi-primitive campsite with 4 corrals.

Facilities: The campsite can accommodate several horse trailers. Hitching rail, potable water, picnic table in camp. No toilet in the horse camp, but there is a flush toilet nearby in the Spring Creek day-use area. Hot showers in the family campground on the east side of Highway 97. No campfires without park permission.

Permits: State park fee

Season: April through October

Contact: Collier Memorial State Park, 800-551-6949, www.oregonstateparks.org/park_228.php,

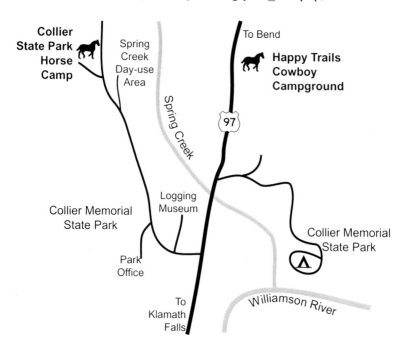

Happy Trails Cowboy Campground

Directions: 30 miles north of Klamath Falls or 100 miles south of Bend on Highway 97, between mileposts 243 and 244. Turn east off Highway 97.
Elevation: 4,200 feet
Campsites: 15 campsites with 30 individual log corrals
Facilities: Flush toilet and portable toilets, hot shower, potable water, fire pits, barbeques, picnic tables, and full hook-ups for one RV. Shared arena and round pen, large fire pit and gathering area for groups.
Permits: None. This is a commercial campground with a fee.
Season: Summer through fall
Contact: www.happytrailscowboycampground.com/, 541-783-3559
Comments: This campground is right next to Highway 97, so you will hear traffic noise from the busy road. However, the camp backs up to the Winema National Forest, so you have access to the Williamson River and Collier State Park plus extensive riding in the national forest without having to cross Highway 97.

*Tex and Shadow frolic in the arena
at Happy Trails Cowboy Campground.*

Collier-Kimball Trail

Trailhead: Start at the Collier State Park horse camp
Length: 20 miles round trip to Kimball State Park, or you can do a 12-mile loop ride by returning on Road 6215
Elevation: 4,200 to 4,600 feet
Difficulty: Easy riding, but the trail is unmarked. Stop by the Collier Park office to pick up a map.
Season: Late spring though fall
Permits: State park fee
Facilities: Parking for several trailers, plus horse corrals and potable water. Toilets in the nearby Spring Creek day-use area. No stock water on the trail until you reach Kimball Park. No horse camping at Kimball Park.

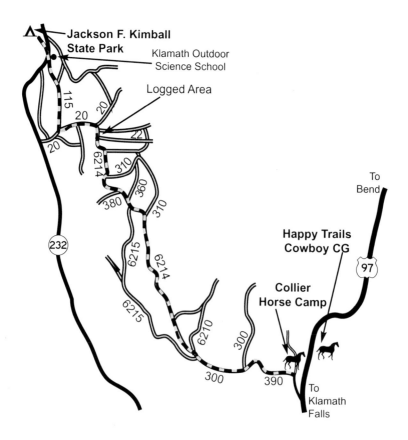

Collier State Park

The Collier-Kimball Trail travels 10 miles (1-way) on forest roads.

Highlights: This trail follows old forest roads through the woods from Collier Memorial State Park to Jackson F. Kimball State Park. The Wood River originates in Kimball Park, where a huge spring flows out of the hillside and creates a full-size river within just a few hundred yards. It's impressive. This trail is not marked and most of the forest roads are unsigned, so stop by the Collier Park office to get a map with the route highlighted. A GPS or compass is recommended.

The Ride: Take Road 390 from the south end of the Collier horse camp and follow it 1.1 miles, then turn left on Road 300. Continue 0.9 mile to the junction with Roads 6210 and 6215. Go right on Road 6210 and ride 0.2 mile, then turn left on Road 6214. Follow Road 6214 for 3.6 miles to the second junction with Road 6215. If you want to make a shorter loop, turn left here onto Road 6215 and follow it back to the junction with Road 300. Or continue on Road 6214 another 2.2 miles until it T-bones into Road 20. Turn left on Road 20 and follow it 0.4 mile down a steep hill, then continue 0.3 mile and turn right on Road 115. In 0.8 mile the road forks. Stay to the left and continue 0.4 mile to the site of the Klamath Outdoor Science School. Skirt the school and cross Hwy. 232 to enter Jackson F. Kimball State Park. Ride a short distance into the park to reach the amazing headwaters of the Wood River.

Rimrock Overlook

Trailhead: Start at Happy Trails Cowboy Campground
Length: Approximately 14 miles round trip. There are several possible routes to the rimrock, so the actual length of the ride depends on which route you take and how far along the rimrock you ride.
Elevation: 4,200 to 4,600 feet
Difficulty: Moderate. Steep drop-offs along the rimrock. If you hate heights stay on Road 9734, which also offers good views.
Season: Late spring though fall
Permits: None
Facilities: The campground has toilets, water, and many other amenities. Water is available on the trail.

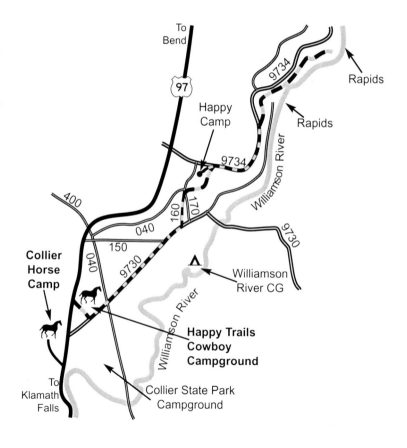

Julie on Persius, Whitney on Shadow, Debbie on Mel, and Suzi on Frosti, on the rimrock trail.

Highlights: The views from the rimrock overlooking the Williamson River valley are breathtaking. In addition to the lovely forest and the Williamson River below, on a clear day you can see both Mt. McLoughlin and Mt. Shasta.

The Ride: Pick up the trail on the southeast edge of Happy Trails Cowboy Campground and follow it 0.3 mile, then turn left on Forest Road 9730 and ride 1.5 mile to Road 160. Turn left and follow it 0.4 mile, then turn right on a single-track trail just before the road begins to climb the ridge. Follow the single-track trail 0.5 mile to the top of the ridge, veer left, and follow a well-defined trail 0.2 mile to Happy Camp. This primitive camp is a nice spot for lunch, with its views of the Cascade peaks and the river valley below. From Happy Camp, retrace your steps past the trail you came up on, and you will shortly reach Road 9734. It parallels the rimrock and provides nice views of the river below, but the most spectacular views can be had by veering off Road 9734 after 0.3 mile and following the trail along the rim. After 2.5 miles there is a viewpoint for the cascades on the Williamson River below. To return to the horse camp, retrace your steps.

Spring Creek Headwaters

Trailhead: Start at the Collier State Park horse camp
Length: 7.5 miles round trip
Elevation: 4,200 to 4,250 feet
Difficulty: Easy
Season: Late spring though fall
Permits: State park fee
Facilities: Parking for several trailers at the horse camp, plus horse corrals and potable water. Toilets in the nearby Spring Creek day-use area. Stock water on the trail at the Spring Creek headwaters.

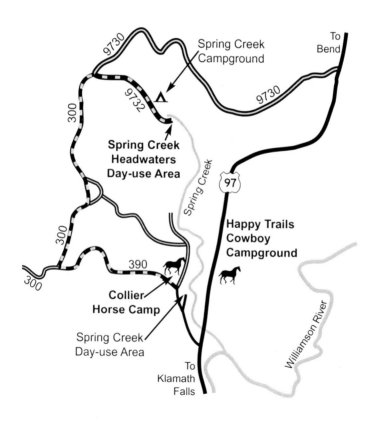

Collier State Park 63

Highlights: This is an easy ride on forest and gravel roads that take you to the huge spring that creates the lovely Spring Creek. The trail is unmarked, though, and the forest roads are not signed until you get near the Spring Creek campground. Stop by the Collier State Park office to pick up a map. Helpful hint: after you turn onto Road 300, at all junctions just make sure you stay on the road that has been more heavily traveled by automobile, and you'll easily find Road 9732.

The Ride: Take Road 390 at the south end of the Collier Park horse camp and follow it 1.1 miles, then turn right on Road 300. Continue 1.85 miles and turn right on Road 9732, a wide gravel road. Ride along it for 0.8 mile, past the entrance to the Spring Creek campground to the Spring Creek Headwaters Day-use Area and the spring itself.

The beautiful Spring Creek flows near Collier Horse Camp. It's an easy ride to the huge spring that creates the creek.

Williamson River Trail

Trailhead: Start at Happy Trails Cowboy Campground
Length: If you take the northern trail it is 5 miles round trip from the horse camp to Williamson River campground, or 7.5 miles round trip to the bridge. If you take the southern route it is 10.2 miles round trip to the bridge. Longer rides are possible.
Elevation: 4,200 feet
Difficulty: Easy
Season: Late spring though fall
Permits: None
Facilities: The campground has toilets, water, and many other facilities. Water is available on the trail.

Highlights: The Williamson River Trail follows the Williamson River from Collier Campground to Williamson River Campground. It's a

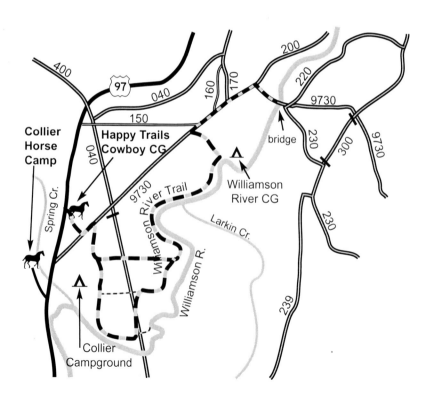

very pretty and relaxing ride, with several possible variations depending on how far you want to ride.

The Ride: Pick up the trail on the southeast edge of Happy Trails Cowboy Campground and follow it 0.3 mile, then turn left on Forest Road 9730 and ride 0.1 mile. Turn right on a small dirt road and continue 0.3 mile until you pass through an opening in a barbed-wire fence and come to a wide trail. If you turn to the right, you'll skirt the park's campground and in 0.6 mile you'll reach the river. From there you can ride along the river nearly 3 miles to the Williamson River Campground. Alternatively, turn left and follow the trail along the fence for 0.7 mile to intersect with the Williamson River Trail. Veer left to go to Williamson River Campground or turn right to loop south and then back toward Collier Campground. Horses are not permitted in either of the campgrounds. From the Williamson River Campground, you can turn left on the entrance road and follow it 0.5 mile, turn right on Road 9730, ride 0.2 mile, and then turn right on a gravel road that leads to a bridge that provides access to the myriad roads and trails on the east side of the Williamson River.

*Lydia on Shadow and Connie on Princess,
strolling along the Williamson River Trail.*

A mule is just like a horse, but even more so.

Pat Parelli

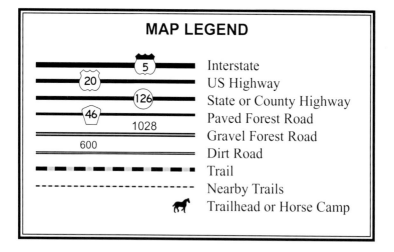

Elijah Bristow State Park

Eugene, Oregon

Elijah Bristow was the first pioneer settler in Lane County, and founder of the town of Pleasant Hill. The park named after him does a remarkable job of preserving the wonderful things about this area that may have attracted Bristow to it in the first place: diverse wildlife, beautiful meadows, lovely forest, and lush marshes.

Located about 14 miles east of Eugene, Elijah Bristow State Park is a great place for a day ride. The park has 14 miles of trails, and horses are permitted on over 10 miles of them. These trails provide access to wildlife viewing sites, lovely forest, and the Middle Fork of the Willamette River. The River Trail in the park is part of the Eugene to Pacific Crest Trail that runs from Alton Baker Park to the PCT near Waldo Lake.

Della, Van and Dancer enjoy the river view.

Elijah Bristow State Park

Directions: From Eugene, take I-5 south to exit 188-A and follow Highway 58 (Willamette Highway) toward Klamath Falls/Oakridge. After 10 miles, turn left on Rattlesnake Road. Drive 0.2 mile and turn right on Wheeler Road. The equestrian trailhead parking area is on the left in 0.3 mile.

Elevation: 620 feet

Campsites: No overnight camping permitted

Facilities: Toilets, drinking water, garbage cans, 4 corrals, 60-foot round pen, plenty of parking for many trailers. Group shelter with picnic tables, fire pit, and 2 barbecues. Part-time camp host.

Permits: None

Season: Year round

Contact: Elijah Bristow State Park, 800-551-6949, www.oregonstateparks.org/park_83.php,

Della is riding Van and ponying Dancer on a forested stretch of the Elk Trail.

Getting to Elijah Bristow State Park

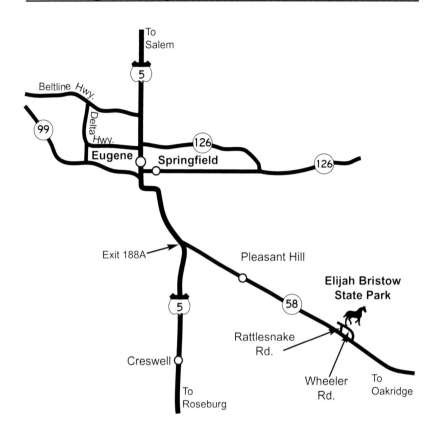

Elijah Bristow Trails

Trail	Difficulty	Elevation	One-Way
Angler's Trails	Moderate	600-645 feet	2 miles
Elk Trail	Easy	600-625 feet	2 miles
Heron Trail	Easy	600-625 feet	1.5 miles
River Trail	Easy	600-660 feet	5 miles

Elijah Bristow State Park Trails

Trailhead: Start at the equestrian parking area off Wheeler Road
Length: 10+ miles of horse trails. Multiple loops are possible.
Elevation: 600 to 660 feet
Difficulty: Easy
Season: Year round, although some trails may be unusable during winter and high-water conditions
Permits: None
Facilities: Toilets, garbage cans, stock water, corrals, round pen, group shelter, and parking for many trailers.
Note: The Turtle Trail and the Oak Nature Trail are for hikers and walkers only.

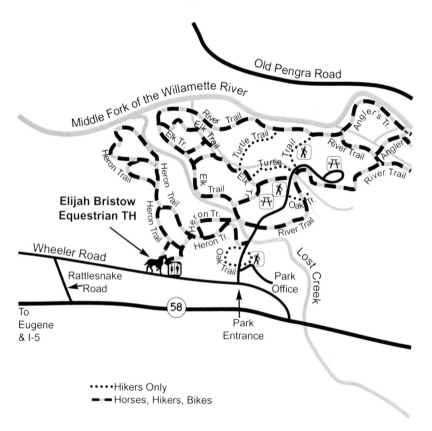

Elijah Bristow State Park

Highlights: Elijah Bristow State Park offers easy, level trails that go through grassy meadows and dense stands of maple and Douglas-fir, past marshes and sloughs, and along the bank of the Middle Fork of the Willamette River. It's possible to create a number of loops, so whether you want to ride all day or take a quick evening jaunt after work, you can tailor your ride to fit the amount of time you have. The wildlife viewing opportunities are exceptional -- keep an eye out for egrets, herons, eagles, turtles, beaver, deer, elk, and coyotes. All this is located just a few miles from Eugene.

The Ride: The majority of the loop trails are located near the equestrian trailhead, while the longer River Trail runs all the way to Dexter Reservoir. Parts of the River Trail may be impassable in winter due to high water. The fords over Lost Creek are similarly off-limits in high-

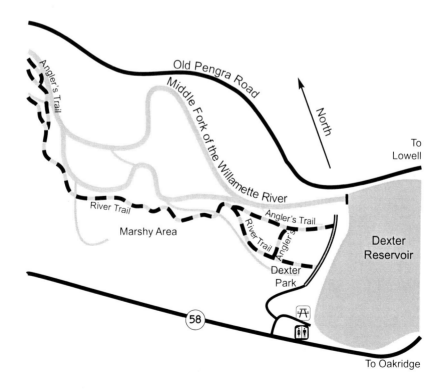

Elijah Bristow State Park (cont.)

water periods. On the other hand, the Elk and Heron Trails are nicely graveled, providing good winter-riding surfaces. The Angler's Trails are not maintained for horses so they can be narrow, brushy, and rocky. They offer close-up views of the river, though, so if you are an experienced rider with a steady mount they are definitely worth exploring. Please keep in mind that all of the trails in the park are multi-user trails, so you'll need to keep an eye out for mountain bikers, or for anglers carrying scary-looking fishing poles.

Della and Van gaze at the Middle Fork of the Willamette River just below the dam at Dexter Reservoir.

Dancer reaches for a bite of grass while Della rides Van along the River Trail.

Dancer checks out some passing hikers as she is ponied by Della and Van on the Angler Trail at Elijah Bristow State Park.

All horses deserve, at least once in their lives, to be loved by a little girl.

Anonymous

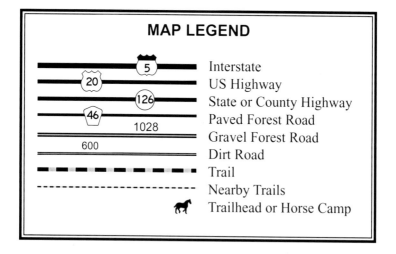

Joe Graham and Clackamas Lake Horse Camps

Mt. Hood National Forest

One of the wonderful things about Joe Graham and Clackamas Lake Horse Camps is their close proximity to Portland -- it's only a 1.5-hour drive to these terrific campgrounds on the south side of Mt. Hood. They are very popular places to horse camp, so make your reservations early. Joe Graham is the main horse camp, but if it is full there are also 19 sites at Clackamas Lake Campground that permit horses. Corrals have been built at several of these sites, but for the others you'll need to high-line or bring a portable corral.

A trip to Joe Graham or Clackamas Lake is worth the advance planning required. Nearby Timothy Lake is a sapphire jewel sitting at the foot of snow-capped Mt. Hood, and the extensive trail network in the surrounding area offers forest solitude along with beautiful vistas of the lake and Mt. Hood. You can circle Timothy Lake, visit Little Crater Lake, or ride north or south on the Pacific Crest Trail. And despite the area's popularity with campers, hikers, and boaters, the trails are relatively uncrowded.

Mt. Hood across Timothy Lake

Getting To Joe Graham/Clack. Lake

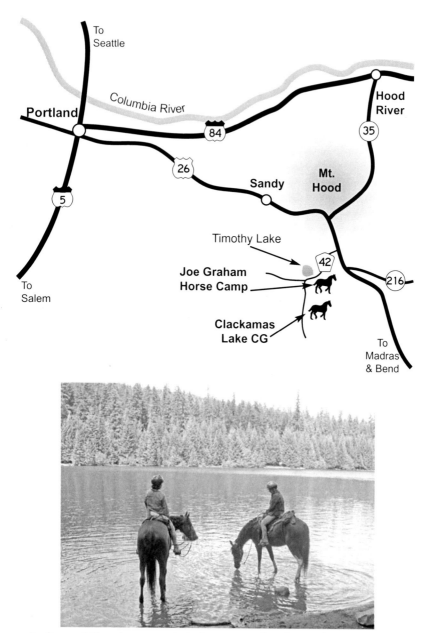

Lydia and Connie water their horses on the shore of Timothy Lake.

Joe Graham/Clack. Lk. Horse Camps

Campground	# Sites	Elevation	Water	Reserv.
Joe Graham HC	14	3,350	Yes	Yes
Clackamas Lake HC	19*	3,350	Yes	Yes

* As of the end of 2008, 6 campsites have corrals. In the near future, corrals will be built in 5 more campsites. The remaining sites require high-lining or a portable corral.

Connie on Diamond and Lydia on Shadow, on the PCT overlooking Timothy Lake.

Joe Graham/Clack. Lake Area Trails

Trail	Difficulty	Elevation	Round Trip
Little Crater Lake Loop	Moderate	3,250-3,500 ft.	10 miles
PCT to Warm Spgs. River	Moderate	3,340-4,300 ft.	16 miles
Timothy Lake Loop	Moderate	3,200-3,400 ft.	15 miles

Joe Graham Horse Camp

Directions: Located 40 miles east of Sandy, 50 miles northwest of Madras, and 45 miles south of Hood River. From Highway 26 turn west on Skyline Road (Road 42). Continue 8.3 miles and turn left into Joe Graham Horse Camp. Day-use parking is along Skyline Road just east of the entrance to the horse camp.

Elevation: 3,350 feet

Campsites: 14 campsites with log corrals

Facilities: Toilets, potable water. Parking for 1 trailer per site.

Permits: Advance reservations required. Go to www.fs.fed.us/r6/centraloregon or call the National Recreation Reservation Service at 877-444-6777. User fee.

Season: May - October

Contact: Zigzag Ranger District, 503-622-7674, www.fs.fed.us/r6/mthood/recreation/campgrounds/index.html

Joe Graham Horse Camp features sturdy 4-horse log corrals.

Clackamas Lake Horse Camp

Directions: Located 40 miles east of Sandy, 50 miles northwest of Madras, and 45 miles south of Hood River. From Highway 26 turn west on Skyline Road (Road 42). Continue 9 miles to the Clackamas Lake Historic Ranger Station. Continue another 0.5 mile past the ranger station and turn left on Road 4270.

Elevation: 3,350 feet

Campsites: 19 sites allow horses. As of the end of 2008, 6 sites have corrals (2-, 3-, or 4-horse) and corrals for 5 more sites are in the works. For the other sites you'll need to highline or bring a portable corral.

Facilities: Toilets, potable water. Parking for 1 trailer per site.

Permits: Advance reservations required. Go to www.fs.fed.us/r6/centraloregon or call the National Recreation Reservation Service at 877-444-6777. User fee.

Season: May - October

Contact: Zigzag Ranger District, 503-622-7674, www.fs.fed.us/r6/mthood/recreation/campgrounds/index.html

One of the sites with corrals at Clackamas Lake campground.

Little Crater Lake Loop

Trailhead: Start at Joe Graham or Clackamas Lake Horse Camp. Day-use parking is available along Skyline Road near the entrance to the camp.

Length: 10 miles round trip

Elevation: 3,250 to 3,500

Difficulty: Moderate

Season: Summer through fall

Permits: User fee for horse camp. No fee for parking on Skyline Road.

Facilities: Toilet and potable water at the horse camp. Stock water is available on the trail.

Highlights: Little Crater Lake is a tiny but remarkable lake. Formed by an artesian spring that gradually eroded the surrounding sand and

Little Crater Lake makes a very nice picnic spot.

silt to create a deep pool, the lake is a brilliant blue and maintains a constant 34-degree temperature year round. The trail to Little Crater Lake runs along the Oak Grove fork of the Clackamas River, then along the shore of Timothy Lake and through lovely stands of old-growth forest. The return trail is hillier and goes through logged areas, so it has less shade but it offers some surprise views of Mt. Hood.

The Ride: From either horse camp, take the connector trail east to the Pacific Crest Trail and turn left. The trail runs along the bank of the Oak Grove fork of the Clackamas River for 1.3 miles, then the trail forks. The left fork goes to South Shore campground. Stay right and follow the PCT along the shore of Timothy Lake. This segment of the trail is generally flat and offers nice views of the lake. After 3.3 miles, trail 537 (the Old 1916 Trail) veers off to the right. This will be your route home, but for now continue straight and after 0.1 mile trail 528 will veer off to the left. Stay right and continue on the PCT 0.4 mile, then turn right on trail 500. After a short distance you will come to hitching posts where you can tie your horses. Continue on foot 0.2 mile to the fascinating Little Crater Lake. For the return trip, return to the junction with trail 537 and turn left to follow it back to the horse camp. This section of the trail includes both dirt roads and single-track trails, and is very well marked.

PCT South to Warm Springs River

Trailhead: Start at Joe Graham or Clackamas Lake Horse Camp. Day-use parking is available along Skyline Road near the entrance to the camp.

Length: 16 miles round trip

Elevation: 3,340 to 4,300 feet

Difficulty: Moderate

Season: Summer through fall

Permits: User fee for horse camp. No fee for parking on Skyline Road.

Facilities: Toilet and potable water at the horse camp. Stock water is available on the trail.

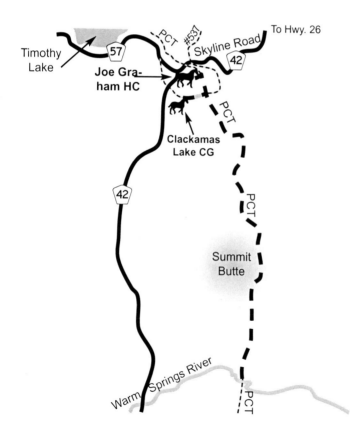

Highlights: The trail follows the Pacific Crest Trail south from Joe Graham Horse Camp through beautiful old-growth forest to the Warm Springs River. The river isn't much more than a creek at this point, but it offers the only place along the trail to water your horse. The highlight of this ride is the lovely forest. The trail travels beneath hemlocks, firs, lodgepole pines, larches, aspen, and vine maples. An added bonus is that the trail is in excellent condition, with very few roots or rocks. While the ride is long, it is relatively easy. And the terrain and vegetation are so varied that you'll want to keep going just to find out what's around the next bend.

The Ride: From either horse camp, take the connector trail heading east that intersects with the Pacific Crest Trail. Turn right on the PCT and ride south 7.8 miles to where the PCT crosses the Warm Springs River. The trail gains over 900 feet as it crosses the shoulder of Summit Butte and then drops nearly 900 feet by the time you reach the river. However, the elevation gain and loss are gradual, with no steep spots along the trail.

Mona on Eclipse and Lydia on Shadow, moving out on the PCT south of Joe Graham Horse Camp.

84 Joe Graham & Clackamas Lake Horse Camps

Timothy Lake Loop

Trailhead: Start at Joe Graham or Clackamas Lake Horse Camp. Day-use parking is available along Skyline Road near the entrance to the camp.

Length: 15 miles round trip

Elevation: 3,200 to 3,400

Difficulty: Moderate

Season: Summer through fall

Permits: User fee for horse camp. No fee for parking on Skyline Road.

Facilities: Toilet and potable water at the horse camp. Stock water is available on the trail.

Highlights: This lovely trail circles Timothy Lake and on a clear day it offers a picture-postcard view of Mt. Hood across the lake. There are numerous places along the way for a picnic on the shore. Seg-

ments of this trail are heavily used by hikers, so be on the lookout. We would classify it as an easy trail except that it is rather long.

The Ride: From Joe Graham take the connector trail to the PCT, turn right, and after 0.5 mile turn right on trail 534 (the Miller Trail). From Clackamas Lake campground, go west on trail 534. Shortly afterward the trail crosses Road 42, and 0.7 mile later it crosses Road 57. In another 0.6 mile you'll meet trail 528. Veer left and follow the trail along the south edge of Timothy Lake, passing several campgrounds. At Hoodview Campground, be sure to ride to the lake edge for a great view of Mt. Hood across the lake. After 2.5 miles the trail reaches the dam that creates Timothy Lake and continues along the west side of the lake. About 1.5 miles beyond the dam, the 0.3 mile spur trail to Meditation Point provides more nice views of the lake. In another 3 miles you'll reach the PCT at the north end of the lake. Turn right and follow the PCT 5 miles back to the horse camps.

*Mona on Eclipse and Lydia on Shadow,
enjoying the view of Mt. Hood across Timothy Lake.*

I never play horseshoes 'cause Mother taught us not to throw our clothes around.

> Mr. Ed
> (The talking horse of the 1960's TV series)

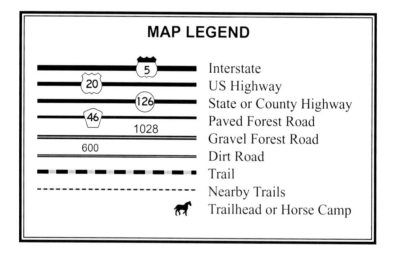

Kelsay Valley Horse Camp

Umpqua National Forest

Kelsay Valley Horse Camp is located about 75 miles east of Roseburg near the crest of the Cascades. It is well equipped for horse camping, and features steel corrals that were hand made by members of the Roseburg chapter of Oregon Equestrian Trails. The camp provides access to the North Umpqua Trail, the Pacific Crest Trail, and several other horse trails in and around the Mt. Thielsen Wilderness. Several loops are possible, and distance riders will be very happy with the area's potential for creating long rides. The beautiful streams, meadows, and lakes in the region can produce a big crop of mosquitoes early in the season, so bring lots of bug spray. We understand the stream fishing nearby is very good. You'll find groceries, gas, and a restaurant at Lemolo Lake Resort, about 5 miles away.

Mt. Thielsen can be seen from several trails in the Kelsay Valley area.

Kelsay Valley Horse Camp

Directions: *From Roseburg,* drive east on Hwy. 138 (exit 124 from I-5) for 72 miles, and turn left at Lemolo Reservoir Junction. Go north on Road 2610, cross the dam, and turn right on Road 2612. Continue 4.25 miles to the junction with Road 60. Veer left, then immediately turn right onto Road 6000-958 and follow it 1.5 miles into camp. *From Bend,* take Hwy. 97 south 76 miles and turn west on Hwy. 138. Continue 27 miles (6 miles past Diamond Lake) and turn right on Road 60, the Windigo Pass Road. Continue 4.6 miles and turn right on Road 6000-958. The horse camp is at the end of the road.

Elevation: 4,300 feet

Campsites: 16 sites. Three sites have 4 corrals, 1 has 3 corrals, 1 has 2 corrals, and 1 has 1 corral. 2 sites have hitching rails only, and the rest can accommodate high-lining. Six sites are pull-throughs that can hold 2 vehicles.

Facilities: Toilet, picnic tables, fire rings, manure pits, camp host. Stock water from nearby creek. No drinking water.

Permits: User fee for camp

Season: Summer through fall

Contact: Diamond Lake Ranger District, 541-498-2531, www.fs.fed.us/r6/umpqua/recreation

Kelsay Valley Area Trails

Trail	Difficulty	Elevation	Round Trip
Calamut Lake	Moderate	4,200-5,900	10-15 miles
Lemolo Lake	Moderate	3,900-4,400	12.6 miles
Maidu Lake	Challenging	4,300-6,000	18 miles
Tenas Peak Loop	Challenging	4,300-6,200	11.7-12.7 mi.
Tenas-PCT-Maidu Loop	Challenging	4,300-6,850	20.5 miles
Windigo Pass	Easy	4,300-5,800	13 miles
Windigo-PCT-Tenas Loop	Challenging	4,300-6,800	16 miles

Getting to Kelsay Valley

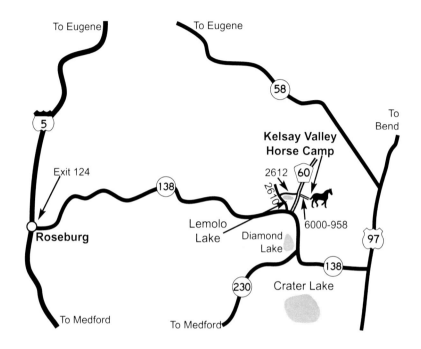

Kelsay Valley has sturdy hand-made steel corrals and a camp host.

Calamut Lake

Trailhead: You can take the trail from the forest camp on Road 6000-958 or you can ride the forest roads to Calamut Lake

Length: 10 miles round trip if you take the trail from the forest camp, or 15.5 miles if you ride the forest roads

Elevation: 4,200 to 5,900 feet

Difficulty: Moderate (assuming the trail from the forest camp has been cleared)

Season: Summer through fall

Permits: None

Facilities: Toilet and picnic tables at Lake Linda. Stock water is available on the trail.

Highlights: The trail that leads directly to Calamut Lake from the forest camp on Road 6000-098 is unsigned, so you'll need to look around for the trailhead. This route goes through an area that was logged just before our visit and the debris had not yet been cleared from the trail,

Small but pretty Lake Linda, on the road route to Calamut Lake.

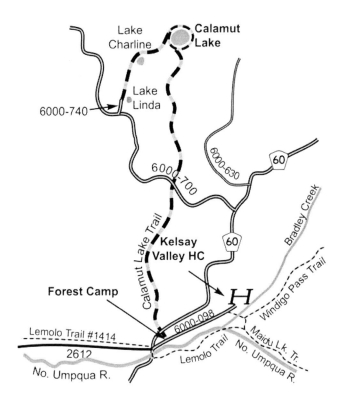

so we took the road route. This alternative route is longer but is an easy ride. It goes through forested and logged areas and has nice views of nearby mountains. Once you reach the hiker trailhead off Road 6000-740, the trail goes past three lovely lakes: Linda, Charline, and Calamut. There is also a trail that circles Calamut Lake.

The Ride: To take the trail to Calamut Lake, head west on Road 6000-098 about 1 mile to the forest camp on the north side of the road. The trail departs from here but is unsigned. To take the road route, go west from the horse camp on Road 6000-098, turn right on Road 60, and continue 2.5 miles. Turn left on Road 6000-700 and after 2 miles turn left on Road 6000-740. In 0.25 mile you'll come to the tiny Lake Linda and a primitive campground that offers a toilet and picnic tables. Continue 0.6 mile farther and Lake Charline appears beside the trail. In another 0.7 mile you'll reach the south end of Calamut Lake. You can circle the lake, which adds another 0.7 mile to the route.

Lemolo Lake

Trailhead: Start at Kelsay Valley Horse Camp
Length: 12.6 miles round trip to White Mule trailhead
Elevation: 3,900 to 4,400 feet
Difficulty: Moderate
Season: Summer through fall
Permits: User fee for the horse camp
Facilities: Toilet and stock water at the horse camp. Stock water is available on the trail.

Highlights: The Lemolo segment of the North Umpqua Trail runs for 2 miles along the beautiful meadows that flank the North Umpqua River. Then it crosses Road 60 and Road 2612 and continues along the mountainside above Lemolo Lake. (When you reach Road 700 about

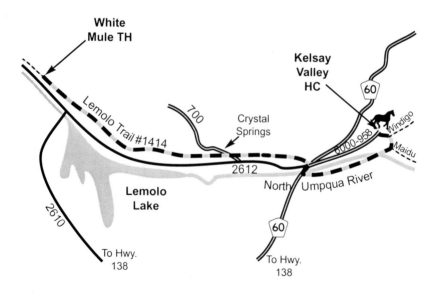

3.5 miles from camp, be sure to take a side trip 0.5 mile north on the 700 road to see the lovely Crystal Springs.) The trail runs above Lemolo Lake all the way to the dam and past it to the White Mule trailhead. The trail offers views of Mt. Thielsen, other nearby peaks, and Lemolo Lake. The North Umpqua Trail continues west from White Mule trailhead.

The Ride: The trail departs from the south side of the road at the entrance to the horse camp. After 0.3 mile the Windigo Pass Trail #1412 goes off to the left. Stay right and in another 0.2 mile the Maidu Lake Trail #1414 goes to the left. Stay right again, and in 0.3 mile you'll cross the North Umpqua River and travel for 1.3 miles next to the flower-filled meadows along its banks. Then the trail reaches Road 60. Turn right and cross the river using the Road 60 bridge, then pick up the trail almost directly across from Road 6000-958 (which goes to the horse camp). From here the trail runs along the mountainside above Road 2612 and Lemolo Lake. There are nice mountain and lake views through the trees.

Teresa leans to avoid a fallen tree as she rides Jane along the bank of the North Umpqua on the Lemolo trail not far from camp.

Maidu Lake

Trailhead: Start at Kelsay Valley Horse Camp
Length: 18 miles round trip
Elevation: 4,300 to 6,000 feet
Difficulty: Challenging: large elevation gain, some downed trees across the trail
Season: Summer through fall
Permits: User fee for the horse camp
Facilities: Toilet and stock water at the horse camp. Stock water is available on the trail.

Highlights: This trail provides access to the Mt. Thielsen Wilderness Area and leads to Maidu Lake, the headwaters of the North Umpqua River. When we rode it in mid-summer 2008, there were a significant

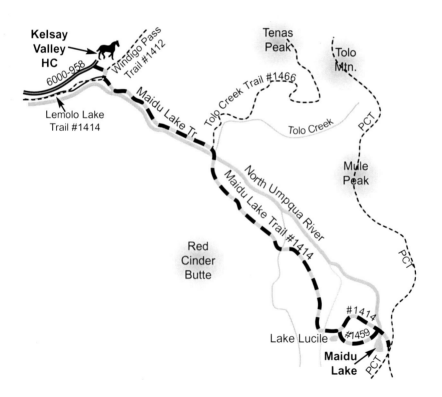

number of downed trees across the trail, even though the trail had been cleared earlier in the season. Given our experience you may need to do some bushwhacking, but overall this is a great trail and it will take you to some lovely High Cascade lakes.

The Ride: The trail departs from the south side of the road at the entrance to the horse camp. After 0.3 mile the Windigo Pass Trail #1412 goes off to the left. Stay right and in another 0.2 mile veer left on the Maidu Lake Trail #1414. (The Lemolo trail goes off to the right.) For the next 2 miles the trail travels along the North Umpqua, initially beside a wide grassy meadow and then along the canyon carved by the creek. After the Tolo Creek Trail #1466 departs on the left, the Maidu Lake Trail enters the Mt. Thielsen Wilderness and moves up the mountainside, away from the river, and through dense timber. The trail gains about 1,500 additional feet of elevation as it climbs toward Lake Lucile and Maidu Lake. You can create a small loop between the lakes by taking the 0.9-mile Lake Lucile Trail #1459 on your return journey. Both Maidu and Lucile Lakes are stocked with trout.

The gang rides out toward Maidu Lake.

Tenas Peak Loop

Trailhead: Start at Kelsay Valley Horse Camp
Length: 11.7 miles round trip, or 12.7 miles if you take the side trail to the summit
Elevation: 4,300 to 6,200 feet (6,500 if you ride to the summit)
Difficulty: Challenging: big elevation gain, many fallen trees across the trail
Season: Summer through fall
Permits: User fee for the horse camp
Facilities: Toilet and stock water at the horse camp. Stock water is available on the trail.

Highlights: We would have given this trail a "Moderate" difficulty rating if it weren't for all the downed timber we encountered across the trail in 2008. Hopefully it will be cleared when you ride it. The trail

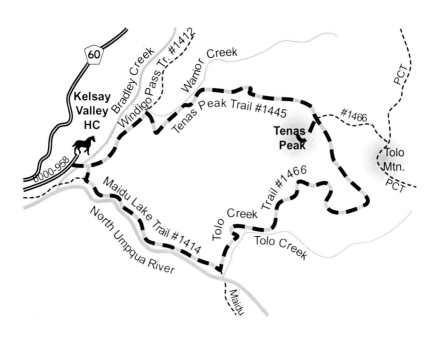

The Tenas Peak trail had lots of downed timber across the trail when we rode it in 2008.

parallels Bradley Creek for a time, then runs along the bank of Warrior Creek through some beautiful old-growth timber. It runs over the shoulder of 6,500-foot Tenas Peak and offers a side trail that climbs 0.5 mile to the summit to see the expansive views. The trail then descends on the Tolo Creek Trail #1466, which offers nice views of nearby mountains. The last leg of the loop returns to camp on the Maidu Lake trail along the North Umpqua.

The Ride: The trail departs from the south side of the entrance to Kelsay Valley Horse Camp. In 0.3 mile the Maidu Lake Trail #1414 goes off to the right. Stay left and in another 1.4 miles turn right on the Tenas Peak Trail #1445, which travels beside Warrior Creek for about a mile. The trail then veers east and climbs to a shoulder near the summit of Tenas Peak. You are about 4.5 miles from camp at this point, and the PCT is 1 mile away. If desired you can take a 0.5 mile detour to the top of Tenas Peak, where a fire lookout used to be. The views are impressive. Then continue on the Tolo Creek Trail #1466 for 4.7 miles as it descends to the bank of the North Umpqua River. Turn right on the Maidu Lake Trail #1414 and ride along the North Umpqua back to camp.

Tenas/PCT/Maidu Loop

Trailhead: Start at Kelsay Valley Horse Camp
Length: 20.5 miles round trip
Elevation: 4,300 to 6,850 feet
Difficulty: Challenging: downed timber, big elevation gains/losses, long trail
Season: Summer through fall
Permits: User fee for horse camp
Facilities: Toilet and stock water at the horse camp. Stock water is available on the trail.

Highlights: If you're looking for a whopper of a ride, this is the one for you. The trail climbs to near the summit of Tenas Peak, then climbs some more to reach the Pacific Crest Trail. While on the PCT you'll

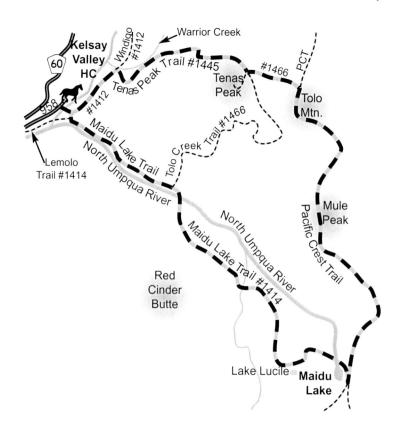

Connie on Diamond, Lydia on Shadow, and Whitney on Dixie, on the Tenas Peak segment of the loop.

go near the peak of Tolo Mountain, over 6,850-foot Mule Peak, and down to Maidu Lake before heading back to camp on the Maidu Lake trail. In some stretches the PCT runs along the county line, so your horse's right feet will be in Klamath County while his left will be in Douglas County. This is a long ride with lots of elevation gain and loss, but you'll see some wonderful views of Cascade peaks and local buttes along the way. For more highlights, see our comments about the Tenas Peak and Maidu Lake trails.

The Ride: The trail departs from the south side of the entrance to Kelsay Valley Horse Camp. In 0.3 mile the Maidu Lake Trail goes to the right. Stay left on the Windigo Pass Trail #1412, then 1.4 mile farther turn right on the Tenas Peak Trail #1445. In 2.8 miles you'll reach the junction with the Tolo Creek Trail #1466 near the summit of Tenas Peak. Turn left on the 1-mile connector trail to the PCT, then turn right on the PCT. While on this 6-mile stretch of the PCT you'll travel near the summit of Tolo Mountain and over Mule Peak, then down to Maidu Lake, gaining and then losing 1,900 cumulative feet of elevation. Whew! This makes the 1,500-foot descent to camp on the Maidu Lake Trail #1414 seem easy.

Windigo Pass

Trailhead: Start at Kelsay Valley Horse Camp
Length: 13 miles round trip
Elevation: 4,300 to 5,800 feet
Difficulty: Easy
Season: Summer through fall
Permits: User fee for the horse camp
Facilities: Toilet and stock water at the horse camp. Toilet at Windigo Pass. Stock water is available on the trail.

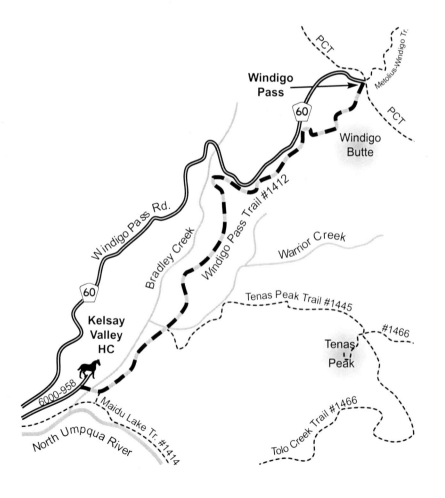

Kelsay Valley Horse Camp 101

Debbie on Split, Connie on Diamond, and Lydia on Shadow enjoying the easy Windigo Pass Trail.

Highlights: The Windigo Pass Trail follows an old forest road (the original road over the pass, perhaps?) for nearly its entire distance. While the trail gains a fair amount of elevation, it's a slow and steady climb the entire way. The trail is nice and wide, so you can trot or canter for long stretches. The trail is shady, its forest views are nice, and in season the rhododendrons blooming along the trail are lovely. It's a great trail for green horses or inexperienced riders, although there is one stream crossing. There are no views from Windigo Pass.

The Ride: The trail departs from the south side of the entrance to Kelsay Valley Horse Camp. In 0.3 mile the Maidu Lake Trail #1414 goes off to the right. Stay left and in another 1.4 miles the Tenas Peak Trail #1445 goes off to the right. Just past this junction there is a creek crossing where you can water your horse. In another 4.8 miles you'll reach Windigo Pass, where you'll find a trailhead parking area and a toilet. The PCT is just a short distance beyond the parking area.

Windigo/PCT/Tenas Loop

Trailhead: Start at Kelsay Valley Horse Camp
Length: 16 miles round trip
Elevation: 4,300 to 6,800 feet
Difficulty: Challenging: downed timber, large elevation gain/loss
Season: Summer through fall
Permits: User fee for the horse camp
Facilities: Toilet and stock water at the horse camp. Stock water is available on the trail.

Highlights: The first segment of this loop, on the Windigo Pass Trail, is easy even though it climbs 1,500 feet. Then while on the PCT segment you'll gain another 1,000 feet in 2.5 miles as you travel toward

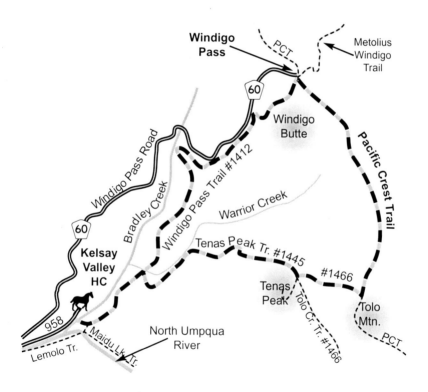

Connie, Debbie, and Lydia ride through an opening in the forest along on the Windigo-PCT-Tenas Loop.

Tolo Mountain. The Tenas Peak segment then descends steadily, and the many downed trees that were across the trail (as of August 2008) made this segment a bit challenging. However, you'll get some terrific views of the surrounding peaks and buttes along the way. For more highlights, see our comments about the Windigo Pass and Tenas Peak trails.

The Ride: The trail departs from the south side of the road at the entrance to Kelsay Valley Horse Camp. In 0.3 mile the Maidu Lake Trail #1414 goes off to the right. Stay left and in another 1.4 miles the Tenas Peak Trail #1445 goes off to the right. Continue left, and in another 4.8 miles you'll reach Windigo Pass, where you'll find a trailhead parking area and a toilet. The Pacific Crest Trail is just a short distance beyond the parking area. Turn right on the PCT and follow it 3.7 miles, then turn right on the Tolo Creek Trail #1466, which will take you to the Tenas Peak Trail #1445 in 1.0 mile. Turn right on the Tenas Peak Trail and follow it back to camp.

The daughter who won't lift a finger in the house is the same child who cycles off madly in the pouring rain to spend all morning mucking out a stable.

Sarah Armstrong

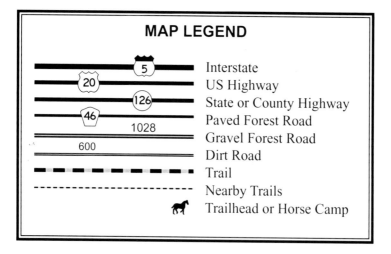

L.L. (Stub) Stewart State Park

Hares Canyon Horse Camp, Buxton, OR

L.L. (Stub) Stewart State Park is the first new state park in Oregon in over 30 years. Built with lottery profits and located about 35 miles west of Portland, the park has a wonderful horse camp. It has over 15 miles of forest trails plus access to the 21-mile Banks-Vernonia State Trail. Hares Canyon Horse Camp is state of the art, with full RV hookups, flush toilets, and hot showers. The campsites are level and nicely graveled, with 4- or 6-horse corrals that have high center poles to accommodate a tarp roof if you want to put one up. Tall trees provide shade on sunny days. The nearby Clayhill Horse Staging Area provides excellent accommodations for day riders as well. In addition to the luxury of Hares Canyon Horse Camp, you'll find plenty of riding opportunities at Stub Stewart State Park.

Hares Canyon Horse Camp has RV hookups and hot showers.

Hares Canyon Horse Camp

Directions: Located about 35 miles west of Portland in L.L. (Stub) Stewart State Park. From the junction of Hwy. 217 and Hwy. 26 west of Portland, travel west on Hwy. 26 for 25 miles and turn right on State Road 47. Continue 4 miles and turn right into the park. The horse camp is at the end of the road, about 1.75 miles from the entrance. The road is paved to the horse camp.

Elevation: 1,250 feet

Campsites: 14 sites with corrals for 4 horses each, and 2 group sites with 6-horse corrals. All sites are back-in, level, and graveled, with full RV hookups and room for 2 vehicles.

Facilities: Flush toilets, potable water, hot showers, manure bins, camp host, and firewood for sale. All sites have fire pits and picnic tables.

Permits: User fees for camping or day use. You can pay at the welcome center or at the fee stations in the horse camp and the Clayhill day use area. Reservations required.

Season: Year-round

Contact: Reservations at 800-452-5687, information at 503-324-0606, www.oregonstateparks.org/park_255.php

Jane and Plum enjoy the accommodations at Hares Creek.

Getting to Stub Stewart State Park

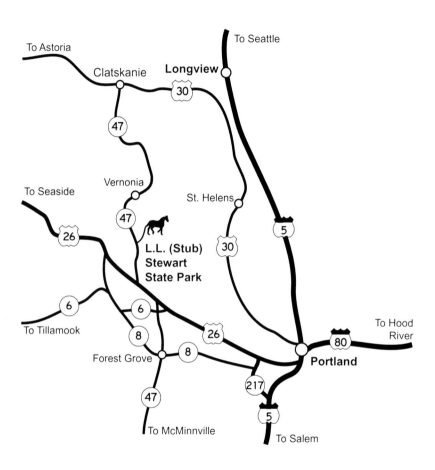

Stub Stewart State Park Trails

Trail	Difficulty	Elevation	Round Trip
Banks-Vernonia Trail	Moderate	200-1,050	up to 42 miles
Hares/B-V Loop	Moderate	1,250-710	5.5 miles
Holli's/Bumping Knots Lp	Moderate	1,250-300	9 miles

Banks-Vernonia State Trail

Trailhead: Start at Hares Canyon Horse Camp or the Clayhill Horse Staging Area at Stub Stewart State Park, or at the Vernonia, Beaver Creek, Tophill, Buxton, or Manning trailheads

Length: 21 miles one way, with 3.5 miles of the trail within the borders of L.L. (Stub) Stewart State Park

Elevation: 200 to 1,050 feet

Difficulty: Moderate -- heavy bicycle traffic on adjacent paved path

Season: Year-round

Permits: Day-use or camping fee for state park

Facilities: Toilets, potable water, and manure bins at the horse camp and the day-use area. No water is available on the trail.

Highlights: The Banks-Vernonia State Trail follows an abandoned railroad bed that dates back to the 1920's. Originally used to haul lumber, freight and passengers from Vernonia and Keasey to Portland, the railroad was later used as a steam excursion train and was abandoned

Catherine on Shane, Jamie on Casey, Maria on Jessie, and Gloria on Devon, traveling the Banks-Vernonia Trail.

L.L. (Stub) Stewart State Park / Hares Canyon Horse Camp

in 1973. The trail runs through beautiful forested terrain and features 12 bridges plus it passes two 80-foot high, 600-foot long wooden railroad trestles. The trail is paved for hikers and bicyclists, with a 3-foot wide bark chip trail for horses beside it.

The Ride: From within L.L. (Stub) Stewart State Park, you can pick up the Banks-Vernonia (B-V) Trail by taking the Boomscooter Trail from the Clayhill Horse Staging Area. (See the map on the next page for more details.) This will connect you to the B-V Trail near where it enters the park on the north end. Heading south, the trail goes gently but steadily downhill until it exits the park 3.5 miles later. The biggest hazards you will encounter on this trail are the bicyclists using the paved portion of the trail. Many cyclists are understandably sensitive about horse manure on the pavement, so please keep your horses on the chip trail. If your horse should happen to poop on the paved path, please be a good neighbor and dismount and kick your meadow muffins off the pavement.

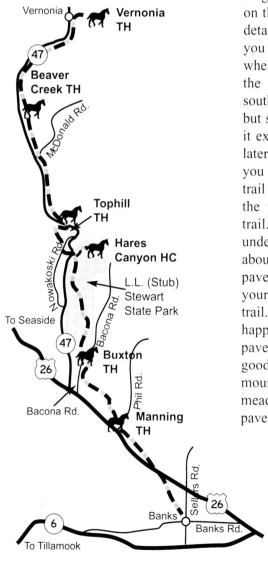

110 L.L. (Stub) Stewart State Park / Hares Canyon Horse Camp

Hares Canyon/B-V Loop

Trailhead: Start at Hares Canyon Horse Camp or the Clayhill Horse Staging Area
Length: 5.5 miles round trip
Elevation: 1,250 to 710 feet
Difficulty: Moderate -- some slopes may be slippery when wet
Season: Year-round
Permits: Day-use or camping fee for state park
Facilities: Toilets, potable water, and manure bins at the horse camp and the day-use area. No water is available on the trail.

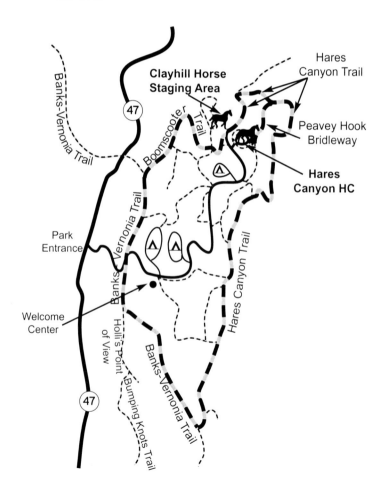

L.L. (Stub) Stewart State Park / Hares Canyon Horse Camp

Highlights: The trail runs downhill through lovely Hares Canyon for several miles, then returns on the Banks-Vernonia trail. The ride is mostly forested with Douglas-fir and alder, with vine maples, sword ferns, salal, oregon grape, and oxalis in the understory. Wild flowers abound in several sunny meadows.

The Ride: Pick up the perimeter trail around the horse camp and ride it to the Peavey Hook Bridleway on the east side of the camp. Veer left and follow the trail downhill for about 0.5 mile to the Hares Canyon Trail. Or you can pick up the Hares Canyon Trail at the Clayhill day-use area. From the junction of Peavey Hook and Hares Canyon, go right and ride the Hares Canyon Trail down through Hares Canyon for about 1.5 miles until the trail meets the Banks-Vernonia Trail. Turn right on the B-V Trail and ride 1.75 miles back up to the Boomscooter Trail, then turn right and continue to the Clayhill horse staging area. From the Clayhill parking area, climb the short gravel trail back to the horse camp. Note that there are 23 trails in the park, many of which are less than a mile in length. To avoid clutter, the map at left doesn't show the names of trails not used on this loop ride. A large and detailed map is available at the park's Welcome Center.

The Hares Canyon Trail features lush vegetation including douglas-fir, alder, vine maples, and sword ferns.

Holli's/Bumping Knots Loop

Trailhead: Start at Hares Canyon Horse Camp or the Clayhill Horse Staging Area
Length: 9 miles round trip
Elevation: 1,250 to 300 feet
Difficulty: Moderate -- some slopes may be slippery when wet
Season: Year-round
Permits: Day-use or camping fee for state park
Facilities: Toilets, potable water, and manure bins at the horse camp and the day-use area. No water is available on the trail.

Highlights: The trail follows the Banks-Vernonia trail to the Holli's Point of View Trail, which runs along the top of a ridge and offers glimpses of the coast range through the trees. Then it follows the Bumping Knots Loop Trail down to a large and very impressive wooden train trestle that is still in use.

The Ride: From the horse camp, ride down to the Clayhill day-use area using the gravel trail that begins directly across the street from the entrance to the horse camp. At the south end of the Clayhill parking

Jamie on Casey, Mariah on Jessie, Gloria on Devon, and Catherine on Shane, at the train trestle on the south end of the Bumping Knots loop.

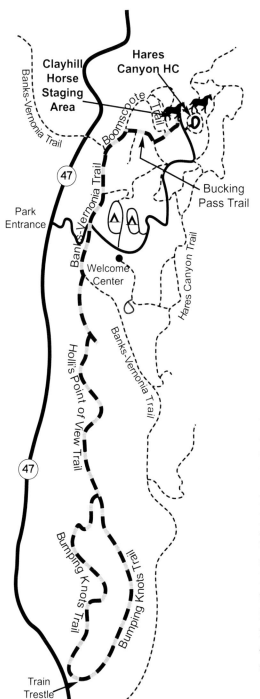

area, pick up the Boomscooter Trail and after a short distance veer left at the junction. In 0.2 mile, turn right on the Bucking Pass Trail and continue another 0.2 mile, then go left on the Boomscooter Trail, which will lead you to the Banks-Vernonia Trail in 0.2 mile. Turn left on the B-V Trail and follow it downhill for 0.8 mile. Pick up the Holli's Point of View Trail on the right and continue 0.4 mile to where a trail departs to the right. Take this fork, as the other trail dead-ends in a short distance. After another mile, the Holli's Point of View Trail intersects with the 2.7-mile Bumping Knots Trail. At the south end of the Bumping Knots loop you'll see a wooden train trestle that is still used by the Tillamook Bay Railroad. Continue around the Bumping Knots loop and return to the horse camp by retracing your steps from there.

Nothing on four legs is quicker than a horse heading back to the barn.

                Pamela C. Biddle and Joel E. Fishman
                All I Need to Know I Learned From My Horse

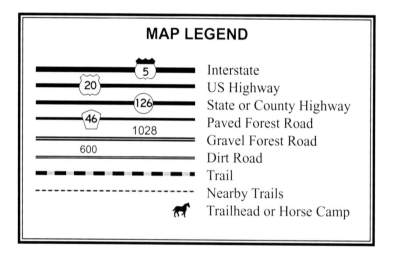

Lost Lake Horse Camp

Mt. Hood National Forest

Lost Lake Horse Camp, located 85 miles east of Portland, is a beautiful, secluded camp that provides access to the Pacific Crest Trail north of Mt. Hood. Lost Lake is very pretty, and the nearby trails provide breathtaking views of Mt. Hood. Give this horse camp a try. You'll enjoy the peace and quiet by night and the remarkable trails by day.

Lost Lake got its name in 1880 when a group of men from Hood River went in search of it. There was some misunderstanding about the route so they had trouble finding the lake. When one of the men observed that the group was lost, another joked that, no, it was the lake that was lost. When they finally found it, they named it Lost Lake. The local Indians called the lake E-e-kwahl-a-mat-yam-lshkt (which means "heart of the mountains"), so it's understandable that the men from Hood River chose to call it something easier to pronounce.

Mt. Hood across Lost Lake.

Lost Lake Horse Camp

Directions: Located 85 miles east of Portland. Drive east on I-84 to Hood River and take exit 64. Head south on Hwy. 35. After 5.4 miles turn right on Ehrck Hill Dr. and follow it 1.8 miles, turn right on Summit Dr. and continue 1.8 miles, then turn left onto the Dee/Hood River Hwy. Follow it 4.2 miles and turn right on Lost Lake Road, then continue 14 miles to Lost Lake. The road is paved all the way to the horse camp. Alternatively, you can take Hwy. 26 east from Portland to Zigzag and drive over Lolo Pass, then turn left on Lost Lake Rd. and continue 7 miles to the lake.

Elevation: 3,200 feet

Campsites: 6 sites with log corrals. Three have 4-horse corrals, one has a 3-horse, and two have 2-horse corrals. Four sites are back-in and 2 are pull-throughs with parking on the edge of the campground road. All sites are for a single vehicle.

Facilities: Toilet, garbage cans, manure bin. Drinking water from spigots next to every other campground.

Permits: User fee for camp. You have to go to the resort store to pay for your site. There is nowhere to turn or park a trailer at the resort store, so you'll either need to walk there or unhitch your trailer and drive.

Lost Lake Area Trails

Trail	Difficulty	Elevation	Round Trip
Jones Creek Road	Easy	2,100-3,300	13 miles
Lost Lake Butte	Moderate	3,200-4,470	5 miles
PCT North	Challenging	3,200-4,500	varies
PCT South	Challenging	3,200-4,100	varies
Walking Trails	Easy	3,200	1.0 or 3.2 mi.

Getting to Lost Lake

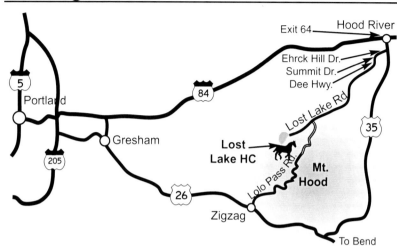

Season: Summer through fall

Contact: Resort: www.lostlakeresort.org or 541-386-6366.
Forest Service: www.fs.fed.us/r6/mthood/recreation/campgrounds.htm or 541-352-6002

Moose grabs a bite to eat at Lost Lake Horse Camp.

Jones Creek Road

Trailhead: Start at Lost Lake Horse Camp
Length: 13 miles round trip
Elevation: 2,100 to 3,300 feet
Difficulty: Easy
Season: Summer through fall
Permits: User fee for horse camp
Facilities: Toilets and drinking water at the horse camp. There is no stock water on the trail.

Highlights: We had heard that there are nice forest roads to explore near Lost Lake, so we decided to try out Jones Creek Road (Forest

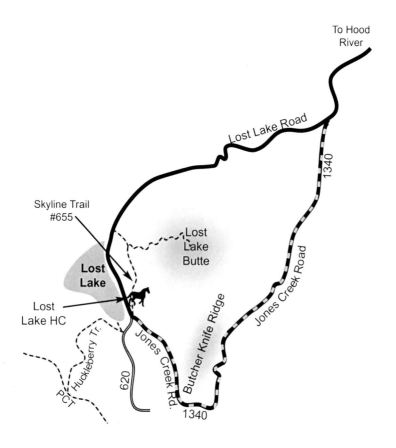

Jones Creek Road offers splendid views of Mt. Hood.

Road #1340). This is an old logging road (now closed to vehicles) that hugs the flank of Butcher Knife Ridge and runs east of Lost Lake Butte. While the Mt. Hood forest map shows the road is gravel, it is actually paved, at least as far as we rode it. If you don't mind riding your horse on crumbling pavement and pushing a few overhanging branches out of the way (the road is not maintained), you'll be rewarded with stunning views of Mt. Hood. When we rode this route in 2008, we reached a point 2.5 miles from camp where an avalanche the previous winter had toppled many small trees across the road. While we probably could have picked our way through the debris and continued, we decided to return to camp and cook dinner instead.

The Ride: Pick up the connector trail behind the horse camp's upper campsites, which will take you to the Skyline Trail. (See the Walking Trails map at the end of this chapter.) Turn right and in 0.25 mile you'll come out at the intersection of the campground road with Road 620 and Jones Creek Road. Turn left onto Jones Creek Road. The entrance is partially blocked to stop vehicles but horses can enter easily. The best views of Mt. Hood can be found about 2 miles from camp.

Lost Lake Butte

Trailhead: Start at Lost Lake Horse Camp
Length: 5 miles round trip
Elevation: 3,200 to 4,470 feet
Difficulty: Moderate
Season: Summer through fall
Permits: User fee for horse camp
Facilities: Toilets and drinking water at the horse camp. There is no stock water on the trail.

Highlights: This trail gains 1,000 feet of elevation in 1.5 miles, but the climb is worth it. Rhododendrons grow profusely under a canopy

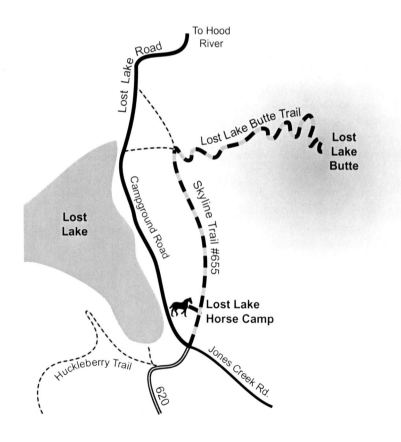

of Douglas-fir, creating a froth of pink in early summer. And the views from the summit are amazing. You can see Mt. Hood, of course, from the top of this 4,470-foot butte. Plus you'll have good views of Mt. Adams, Mt. Rainier, Mt. Jefferson, and Mt. St. Helens. Looking off to the east you can see the Hood River valley and the Columbia Gorge. Dazzling.

The Ride: Pick up the connector trail behind the horse camp's upper campsites, which will take you to the Skyline Trail. (See the Walking Trails map at the end of this chapter.) Turn left and follow the Skyline Trail for 1 mile, then turn right on the Lost Lake Butte Trail. You'll climb steeply, and in another 1.5 miles you'll arrive at the summit. The lower part of the trail is rather rocky, but the higher you go the fewer rocks there are. Wonderful views await you at the top.

Lydia and Shadow take in the view of Mt. Hood from the top of Lost Lake Butte.

Pacific Crest Trail North

Trailhead: Start at Lost Lake Horse Camp
Length: 10.5 miles round trip to Buck Peak, 21 miles round trip to Indian Springs
Elevation: 3,200 to 4,500 feet
Difficulty: Huckleberry Trail is challenging, PCT is moderate
Season: Summer through fall
Permits: User fee for horse camp
Facilities: Toilets and drinking water at the horse camp. Stock water is available on the trail.

Highlights: The 2-mile Huckleberry Trail that takes you to the Pacific Crest Trail is challenging, since it climbs fairly steeply (gaining 800

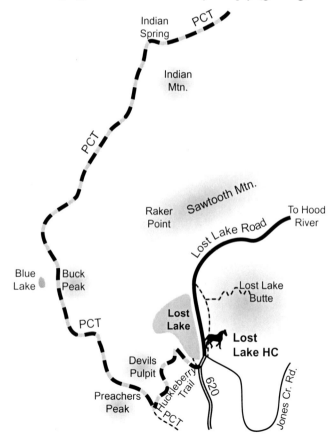

feet in 2 miles) and traverses several steep hillsides. Once you reach the PCT, however, the going is much easier. The trail is nice and wide, with few steep traverses. You'll have good views of Lost Lake, Sawtooth Mountain, Raker Point, Mt. Adams, and Mt. St. Helens. When you first turn onto the PCT, you'll pass between Preachers Peak and Devils Pulpit (opposing forces, perhaps?). There is one spot on the Huckleberry Trail where you can water your horses year round. Early in the season you'll find several water spots along the trail.

The Ride: Pick up the connector trail behind the horse camp's upper campsites, which will take you to the Skyline Trail. (See the Walking Trails map at the end of this chapter.) Turn right and follow it 0.25 mile to the junction of the campground road with Road 620 and Jones Creek Road. Continue straight ahead on Road 620 for 0.25 mile and the trailhead will be on the right. The trail splits just past the trailhead sign, with the trail to the right going down to the lake. Veer left to pick up the Huckleberry Trail. Follow it uphill 2 miles, then turn right on the PCT. From here to Indian Springs there isn't much elevation gain/loss and there are only a few spots with steep slopes to cross.

Lydia on Shadow, Connie on Diamond, and Ray on Moose heading north on the PCT.

Pacific Crest Trail South

Trailhead: Start at Lost Lake Horse Camp
Length: 13.5 miles round trip to Lolo Pass
Elevation: 3,200 to 4,100 feet
Difficulty: Challenging--very steep side hills
Season: Summer through fall
Permits: User fee for the horse camp
Facilities: Toilet and stock water at the horse camp. Stock water is available on the trail.

Highlights: The Huckleberry Trail is a challenge, with its significant elevation gain and steep traverses. The section of the PCT that runs south from here is also challenging, for while it doesn't gain or lose much elevation, several of the slopes you must traverse can be daunting. When you come to a section like this, the only thing to do is

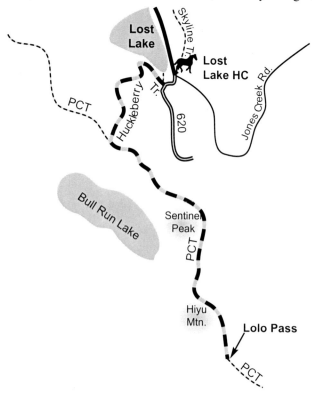

This section of the PCT traverses some very steep slopes, but the views of Mt. Hood are breathtaking.

"Cowboy Up," as my friend Ray says, "and get off and walk." On the positive side, the views of Mt. Hood on this section of the trail are stunning.

The Ride: Pick up the connector trail behind the horse camp's upper campsites, which will take you to the Skyline Trail. (See the Walking Trails map at the end of this chapter.) Turn right and follow it 0.25 mile to the junction of the campground road with Road 620 and Jones Creek Road. Continue straight ahead on Road 620 for 0.25 mile and the trailhead will be on the right. The trail splits just past the trailhead sign, with the trail on the right going down to the lake. Veer left to pick up the Huckleberry Trail. Follow it uphill 2 miles, then turn left on the PCT. Once you reach the PCT there isn't much elevation gain or loss, but as you travel across Sentinel Peak and Hiyu Mountain, the traverses are extremely steep. In one spot you cross a rock face where the trail has literally been hacked out of the cliff. While the trail is as wide as normal, the sheer drop down and the vertical rock face on the uphill side create a very difficult spot to ride if you don't like heights. Other than these steep traverses the trail is quite moderate difficult, and there are some stunning views of Mt. Hood going out, and great views of Mt. Adams on the way home.

Walking Trails

Trailhead: The Lakeshore Trail can be accessed from any campground or from the junction of the Huckleberry Trail and Road 620. The Old Growth Trail runs from the organization camp across from the horse camp to the Loop A campsites and can be accessed from the organization camp, the road into/out of the Loop F campsites or across from the entrance to the Loop A campsites. Horses are not allowed on these trails.

Length: Lakeshore Trail: 3.2 miles
Old Growth Interpretive Trail: 1 mile

Elevation: 3,200 feet

Difficulty: Easy

Season: Summer through fall

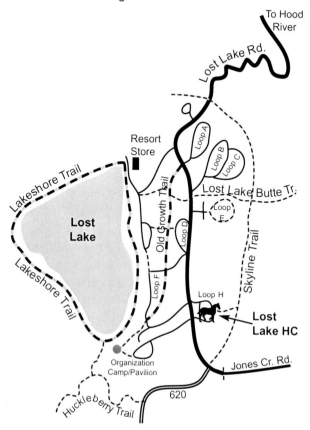

Ray and Connie take a leisurely walk on the Lakeshore Trail.

Permits: User fee for horse camp

Facilities: Toilet and potable water at the horse camp. No water is available on the trail.

Highlights: OK, I know this book is supposed to be about horse trails, but Lost Lake has some really nice walking trails nearby as well. Horses are not allowed on these trails. Whether you are stretching your legs or walking your dog, the trails give you a nice close-up look at the lake and the surrounding forest.

The 3.2-mile Lakeshore Trail around the lake runs along the shoreline and provides continuous views of and access to the lake. At the north end you'll have a beautiful view of Mt. Hood looming over the lake. The trail is either gravel or boardwalk, depending on the terrain.

The Old Growth Interpretive Trail is a mile-long wheelchair-accessible boardwalk. It has interpretive signs every few hundred feet that tell about the enormous old-growth trees near the trail and the plants and animals that thrive within this ancient ecosystem.

Never give up. For fifty years they said the horse was through. Now look at him—a status symbol.

> Fletcher Knebel

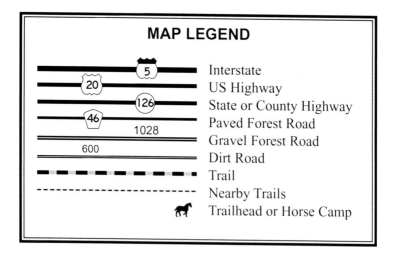

Mildred Kanipe Memorial Park

Oakland, Oregon

Mildred Kanipe (rhymes with "ripe") was born in 1907 near Oakland, Oregon, in the same house where her mother was born. She lived her entire life in that house and never married, making her living raising dairy cows, beef cattle, horses, sheep, goats, rabbits, chickens, hay, grain, fruit, and nuts. Over the years she acquired several adjacent properties, and when she died in 1983 she willed her nearly 1,100-acre ranch to Douglas County with the requirement that it become a public park with equestrian trails.

Today the park offers 5 main loop trails with numerous other connecting trails that allow horseback riders to explore the old growth Douglas-fir forests, oak savannahs, and sunlit meadows of this historic ranch. The forested hilltops provide expansive views, and wild flowers bloom in season. While the park has no overnight camping facilities at this time, it offers wonderful day-riding opportunities.

Midge on Superr and Lois on Mika in a meadow at Kanipe Park.

Mildred Kanipe Memorial Park

Directions: Located 24 miles north of Roseburg, or 52 miles south of Eugene. *From Roseburg*, take I-5 north 13 miles to the Oakland exit (#138). Merge onto Stearns Lane and follow it 1.4 miles. Turn left on Hwy. 99, and in 0.1 mile turn right on Locust St. (Hwy. 22), which becomes Driver Valley Road. Follow it for 4 miles, then turn left on the Medley-Elkhead Road (Hwy. 50) and continue 3 miles to the park. *From Eugene*, take I-5 south 38 miles to the Elkhead/Yoncalla exit (#154). Turn left on Elk Head Road (Hwy. 25), and in 0.3 mile turn left on Elkhead Road (Hwy. 7 at that point, but it becomes Hwy. 50). Follow it 12 miles to the park.

Elevation: 625 feet

Campsites: No overnight facilities at this time, but the County may consider permitting horse camping in the future.

Facilities: Huge equestrian parking area, toilet, stock water in season, group shelter with picnic tables. Additional picnic area at Kanipe homesite with access to trails for hikers.

Permits: None. Dogs not allowed in the park except on leash in the homesite area.

Season: Day use only. Open to horses March 16 - October 31.

Contact: Douglas County Parks, 541-459-9567 www.co.douglas.or.us/parks/parktour.asp

The grass parking area at the Kanipe Park trailhead, with the group shelter and Ben More Mountain in the background.

Getting to Kanipe Park

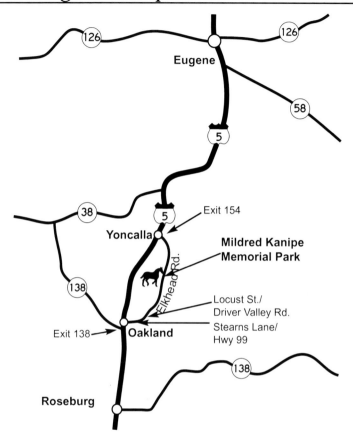

Kanipe Park Area Trails

Trail	Difficulty	Elevation	Round Trip*
Fern Woods Loop	Easy	540-850	~ 3.5 miles
Mildred's Forest Loop	Easy	540-800	~ 3.2 miles
Oak Savannah Loop	Easy	550-760	~ 2.3 miles
School House Loop	Easy	550-625	~ 2.0 miles
Underwood Hill Loop	Moderate	540-875	~ 3.0 miles

* All mileage is from the trailhead, around the loop, and back to the trailhead.

Mildred Kanipe Park Trails

Trailhead: Start at the equestrian trailhead at Mildred Kanipe State Park, 7 miles northeast of the town of Oakland.

Length: Varies. There are 5 marked loop trails in the park, plus a number of unmarked trails and dirt roads you can use to explore the park.

Elevation: 540 to 875 feet

Difficulty: Most of the trails are easy, although the trails in the Underwood Hill area have some fairly steep sections. Some possible muddy areas where the trails cross trickling streams. Watch for poison oak.

Season: March 16 - October 31

Permits: None

Facilities: Toilets and group shelter with picnic tables at equestrian trailhead, stock water in season at the trailhead. Picnic tables at Kanipe homesite. Stock water is available from Bachelor Creek.

Highlights: There are riding opportunities in Kanipe Park for everyone, from easy trails suitable for green horses and inexperienced rid-

Lois in Mika and Midge on Superr Starr, as they ride through a meadow on the Mildred's Forest trail.

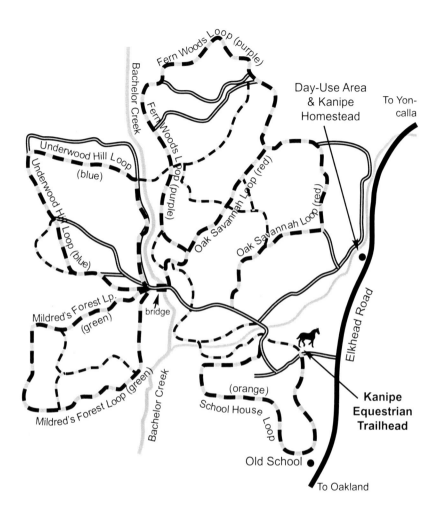

ers to strenuous hill trails that can be used for conditioning rides. On the park's rolling hills you'll find old-growth Douglas-fir stands (including the area locals call "the enchanted forest" at the north end of Fern Woods Loop), sunny meadows, and oak savannahs with a deep carpet of grass beneath. Wildflowers are plentiful and varied.

Be sure to visit the old Kanipe homestead to see the historic 1850's home, barn, and other outbuildings. Mildred Kanipe was a real character who was born here and ranched this property until she died. She loved horses, and the legacy she has created for the equestrian com-

Kanipe Park Trails (continued)

munity is a treasure. For more information on the colorful life of Mildred Kanipe and the history of the land that became the park, see Lois Christiansen Eagleton's book, *"For Love of the Land, the Legacy of Mildred Kanipe."*

The Ride: Kanipe Park offers a variety of trails that allow you to explore the area on your own and make your rides as long or short as you please. There are 5 loop trails marked with colored diamonds painted on the trees, plus plenty of unmarked trails and dirt roads. You can vary your rides by taking the unmarked trails, and since they eventually all intersect with marked trails you can't get lost. The trails in the Underwood Hill section have some steep sections and there are some areas where poison oak can be found. Otherwise the trails are easy. There is a place to water your horses where the connector trail between the Fern Woods and Underwood Hill loops crosses Bachelor Creek.

*The park has rolling hills
that offer expansive views from their summits.*

Mildred Kanipe Memorial Park   135

Midge on Superr and Lois on Mika, enjoying one of the park's oak savannahs, which are among the most extensive in Oregon.

Mildred Kanipe's 1850's-vintage home can be seen in the park. The Friends of Kanipe Park group is working to preserve it, along with the barns and other outbuildings of this historic ranch.

The world is best viewed through the ears of a horse.

Anonymous

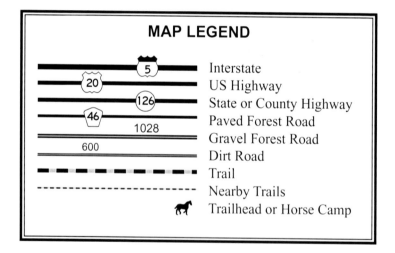

Milo McIver State Park

Estacada, Oregon

Milo McIver was Oregon State Highway Commissioner from 1950 to 1962 and had a big impact on Oregon's road system. The lovely park that is named for him is located on the bank of the Clackamas River about 25 miles southeast of Portland and 3 miles from Estacada. The park has plenty of amenities for the general public, including picnic areas for families or groups, camping facilities, a boat/rafter ramp, and a disc golf course. The park is also very popular with equestrians because of its 7-mile network of trails through the park's forests, along the river, and around meadows and farmland. There are several loop trail options, and you can ride here year round. Horse camping is not permitted in the park.

The Clackamas River flows along the park's northern border.

Milo McIver State Park

Directions: Located about 25 miles southeast of Portland. From I-205, take exit #12A (to Clackamas and Estacada) and drive east on Hwy. 212/224 for 3.2 miles. Turn right on Hwy. 224 toward Estacada, drive 1.1 mile, and veer right on Springwater Road. The road immediately crosses the Clackamas River and turns left. Continue on Springwater Rd. for 9.5 miles and turn left into the park. To reach the equestrian parking area, turn right at the first stop sign and go straight at the second stop, then turn right into the parking area.

Elevation: 600 feet

Campsites: Horse camping is not permitted

Facilities: Portable toilet, garbage cans, picnic tables, hitching posts, mounting block, ADA mounting ramp, arena, stock water spigot with a hose (so you can hose off your sweaty horse). Parking for many trailers.

Permits: Daily use fee or annual fee

Season: Year round

Contact: www.oregonstateparks.org/park_142.php or 503-630-7150

McIver Park Trails

Trail	Difficulty	Elevation	Round Trip*
Southern Loops	Easy	600-700	1.2-1.3 mi.
Short Northern Loop	Moderate	600-350	3.0 miles
Long Northern Loop	Moderate	600-300	3.8 miles
Perimeter Loop	Moderate	700-300	5.0 miles

* Mileages are from the trailhead, around the loop, and back to the trailhead.

Getting to Milo McIver State Park

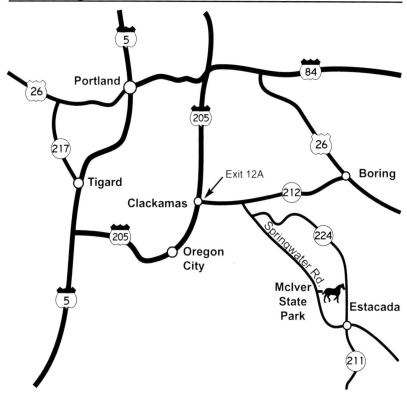

McIver Park has a huge parking area for equestrians.

Milo McIver State Park Trails

Trailhead: At the park's equestrian parking lot
Length: 7 miles of trail in the park, with opportunities to create several loop rides
Elevation: 300 to 700 feet
Difficulty: Moderate--the hills can be slippery in wet conditions
Season: Year round
Permits: Daily or annual use fee
Facilities: Portable toilet, garbage cans, picnic tables, hitching posts, mounting block, ADA mounting ramp, arena, stock water, parking for many trailers.

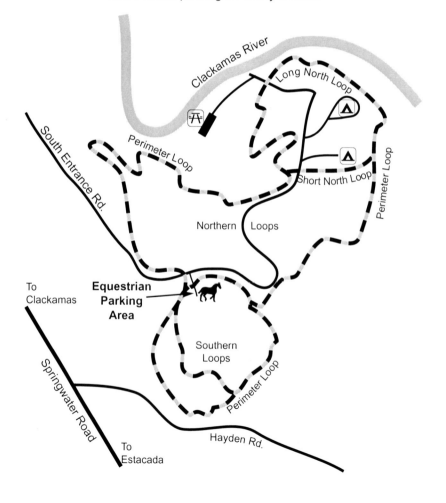

*Cassie and Viset lead the way up the river loop,
with Alex on Cynder following.*

Highlights: McIver State Park's 7 miles of trails provide opportunities for year-round riding. On hot summer days the dense shade of the northern loops provides a cool place to ride and offers views of the Clackamas River. And even in soggy winter conditions, the southern loops have good footing. McIver is a great place for an after-work ride, a quick morning workout, or a leisurely weekend ride.

The Ride: Trails depart from both sides of the equestrian parking lot. The southern loops are 1.2 and 1.3 miles long. They are mostly open terrain, running through meadows and along the edges of cultivated fields. The northern loops descend into the valley carved by the Clackamas River. The shorter loop is 3 miles long, and features an elevation change of about 200 feet, while the longer loop is 3.8 miles long and drops 300 feet to the bank of the Clackamas River before climbing back up to the parking area. If you ride the entire perimeter loop you'll enjoy a 5-mile ride with a 400-foot elevation change. If you ride the northern loops in a counter-clockwise fashion you will take the somewhat more gradual trails downhill and save the steeper slopes for your uphill journey.

McIver State Park (cont.)

Alex on Cynder and Cassie on Viset as they enjoy one of the southern loops.

Cassie and Alex make their way down the trail to the Clackamas River.

Milo McIver State Park 143

*Cassie and Alex at the Clackamas River
on the northern perimeter of the park.*

*While Alex lets Cynder have a nice roll,
Cassie hoses off Viset near the edge of the parking area.*

No hour of life is lost that is spent in the saddle.

Winston Churchill

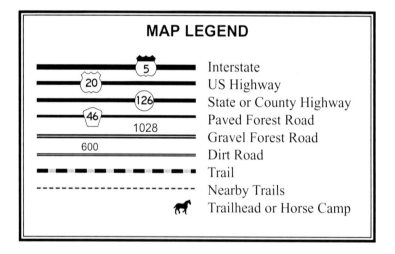

Molalla River Corridor

Molalla, Oregon

Oh, what a wonderful trail system! The Molalla River Corridor offers more than 50 miles of trails over varied terrain, so there's something here for everyone. The Corridor's forest roads and single-track trails provide access to the forested hillsides above the Molalla River. These well-marked non-motorized trails are shared with hikers and mountain bikers. And while the single-track trails are closed in winter, the Huckleberry Trail is open year round. Considering how close the trail system is to major metropolitan areas, it's surprising how remote it feels here. The most popular equestrian trailhead is at Hardy Creek, or you can start at the Yellow Gate trailhead to make it easier to explore the southern part of the corridor.

The Molalla River Corridor trails provide some lovely views of the surrounding area.

Molalla River Corridor

Directions: Located 9 miles southeast of Molalla. *From Portland*, drive south on I-205 toward Oregon City. Take exit 10 (Hwy. 213) and drive 16.8 miles, then turn left on Hwy. 211 and drive into Molalla. *From Salem*, drive north on I-5 and take the Woodburn exit (exit 271). Travel east on Hwy. 211 for 16 miles to Molalla. On the eastern edge of Molalla, turn right on Mathias Rd. In 0.3 mile the road turns sharply left and becomes Feyrer Park Rd. In 1.7 miles this road crosses the Molalla River at Feyrer Park and ends at a "T" intersection. Turn right onto Dickey Prairie Road and continue another 5.4 miles to the Glen Avon bridge. The bridge is on your right just past a 20 mph right turn and just before a Dead End sign. Turn right to cross the bridge and continue south 3.5 miles on Molalla River Road to the Hardy Creek trailhead on the right. The trailhead is unmarked, so look for other horse trailers. The trails can also be accessed using the Yellow Gate trailhead, which is 1.8 miles beyond the Hardy Creek trailhead on the right. The Yellow Gate itself is on the right, and the parking area is on the left side of the road.

Elevation: 700 feet

Campsites: Camping is not permitted in the Molalla River Corridor

Facilities: Toilet and parking for 6-10 trailers at Hardy Creek; parking for 3-4 trailers at the Yellow Gate trailhead

Permits: None

Season: Year round

Contact: 503-375-5646, or www.blm.gov/or/districts/salem/recreation/activities.php

Molalla River Corridor 147

Getting to Molalla River Corridor

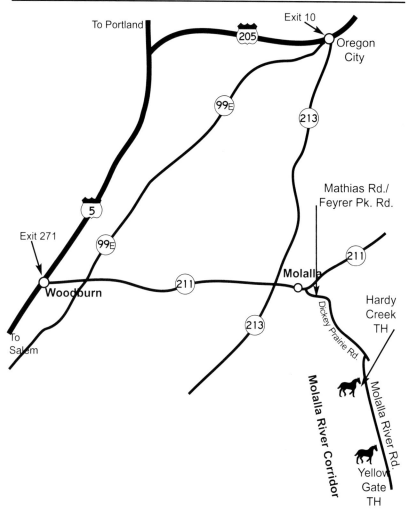

Molalla River Corridor Trails

Trail	Difficulty	Elevation	Round Trip
Huckleberry Trail	Easy	700-1,500	20 miles
Other Molalla River trails	varies	varies	varies

Molalla River Trails

Trailhead: Start at the Hardy Creek trailhead off Molalla Forest Road southeast of Molalla. You can also access the trails from the Yellow Gate trailhead off Molalla Forest Road.

Length: Varies. Several trails to choose from.

Elevation: 700 to 1,500 feet

Difficulty: Varies. Huckleberry Trail is easy. Most single-track trails are easy or moderate, but in a few places the Rim Trail is steep and rocky.

Season: Year round

Permits: None

Facilities: Toilets at the Hardy Creek trailhead. Stock water is available on the trail.

Highlights: The Huckleberry Trail is an old forest road that runs almost the entire length of the corridor and forms the eastern border of the trail system. The Huckleberry Trail is accessible year round, but

Paul on Pete and Stacy on Sonny, enjoying the expansive views from an overlook along the Huckleberry trail.

Molalla River Corridor 149

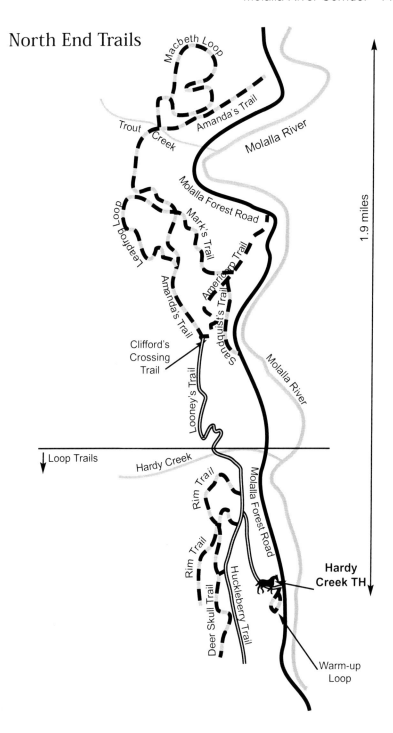

Molalla River Corridor
Loop Trails

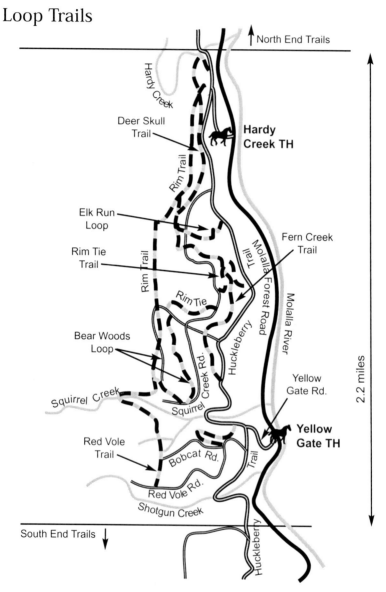

from October to May the side trails are closed to minimize damage to the trails. In summer the side trails are open, providing opportunities for multiple loop rides. These are multi-user trails, so they are shared

Molalla River Corridor 151

South End Trails

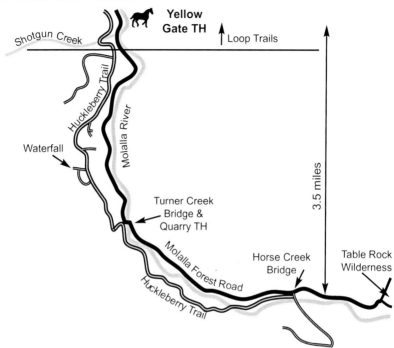

with hikers and mountain bikers. Because the trail system is so long, the map is divided into 3 segments: the North End, the South End, and the Loop Trails segment in between.

The Ride: The North End trails (north of Hardy Creek) appear to have been constructed with mountain bikes in mind, as this area has a number of tight loops and lots of trails packed into a fairly small area. The central Loop Trails area extends from Hardy Creek southward to Shotgun Creek. Several forest roads and trails connect the Huckleberry Trail with the Rim Trail, which runs along the western rim of the canyon. The South End trails run from Shotgun Creek all the way to the Table Rock Wilderness. We haven't done much exploring in the South End because it's so far from the Hardy Creek trailhead, but in the area we've ridden there is a nice waterfall, a beautiful canyon overlook spot, and lots of lovely forest. If you are interested in exploring the south end trails, you may want to park at the Yellow Gate trailhead.

Molalla River Corridor (cont.)

The Hardy Creek trailhead can accommodate 6-8 trailers. There is overflow parking across the road.

The forest along the Molalla River Corridor is beautiful, and the underlying vegetation is lush.

Molalla River Corridor 153

Paul on Pete and Stacy on Sonny as they make their way across Hardy Creek on Amanda's trail.

Paul & Pete and Stacy & Sonny, enjoying the Rim trail.

Anyone who is concerned about his dignity would be well advised to keep away from horses.

Prince Philip, Duke of Edinburgh

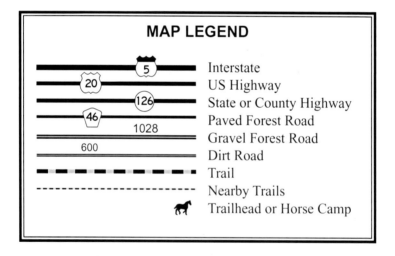

Mt. Pisgah
(Buford Recreation Area)
Eugene, Oregon

When Howard Buford deeded the Mt. Pisgah land to Lane County, he stipulated that the trails must remain available to equestrians. Bless that man -- he did the equestrian community a big favor. Buford's namesake 2,363-acre park is only a short drive from downtown Eugene. It offers several multi-user trails that lead to the top of 1,531-foot Mt. Pisgah and provide great views of the entire south end of the Willamette Valley. The Coast Fork of the Willamette River creates the western border of the park, and the Middle Fork of the Willamette is just north of the park. The trails run through both grassy meadows and forested areas, and riders have plenty of opportunities to create their own loops on the park's many trails.

Della is riding Van and leading Dancer, at the top of Mt. Pisgah.

Mt. Pisgah/Buford Recreation Area

Directions: From Eugene or Springfield, drive south on I-5 and take exit 189 toward 30th Avenue. Merge onto McVay Hwy. and continue 0.6 mile. Turn left at E. 30th Ave., go over the freeway, and turn left on Franklin Blvd. (you'll see signs for Springfield/Fwy. N.). In 0.5 mile turn right at Franklin Blvd. E., then left on Seavey Loop Road. Follow it 1.5 miles, then continue straight on Seavey Way for 0.3 mile. When you reach the park, turn left on Frank Parrish Road, and drive 0.2 mile to the main equestrian trailhead.

A second equestrian trailhead is located at the southeast corner of the park, off Ridgeway Rd. This parking lot is too narrow to turn around in, so you'll need to back in. Go south on I-5 and take exit 188A to merge onto the Willamette Hwy. (Hwy. 58). Continue 4.3 miles and turn left on Ridgeway Rd. Follow it 1.8 miles to the trailhead.

Elevation: 470 feet

Campsites: Overnight camping is not permitted

Facilities: Toilets, garbage cans. Handicapped-access ramp and parking for many trailers at the Frank Parrish Road lot. The Ridgeway Road lot is very small.

Permits: Daily or annual fee

Season: Year round, though some trails are muddy in winter

Contact: www.co.lane.or.us/Parks/MtPisgahPage.htm, 541-682-2000

Getting to Mt. Pisgah

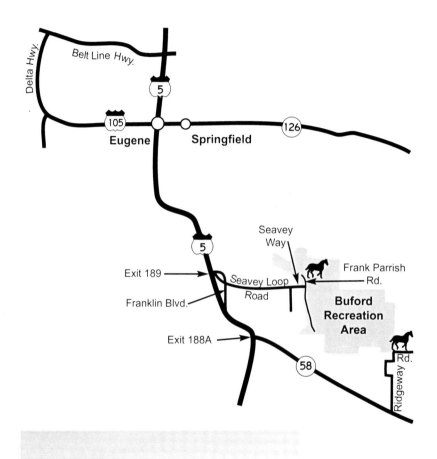

The views from the summit of Mt. Pisgah are stunning.

Mt. Pisgah Trails

Trailhead: Start at the main Mt. Pisgah equestrian trailhead or the trailhead off Ridgeway Road
Length: Varies. Many loop rides are possible.
Elevation: 470 to 1,530 feet
Difficulty: Moderate to challenging. Some trails can be muddy and slick in winter, and several trails have sections that climb steeply. Some trails are rocky, which may be difficult for barefoot horses.
Season: Year round
Permits: Daily or annual fee
Facilities: Toilets, garbage cans. Handicapped-access ramp and parking for many trailers at the Frank Parrish Road lot. The Ridgeway Road lot is very small.

Some of the trails on Mt. Pisgah run through sunny meadows that offer good views of the surrounding area.

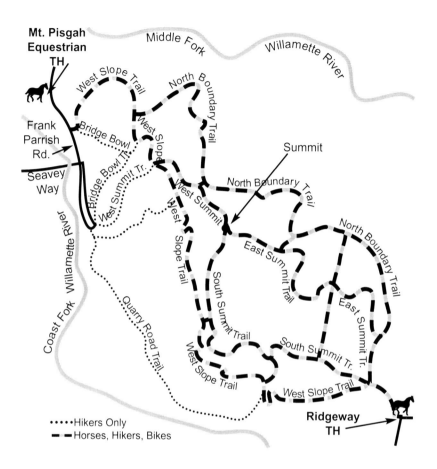

Mt. Pisgah Trails

Trail	Difficulty	Elevation Gain	One-Way
West Summit Trail	Moderate	1,050 feet	1.4 miles
East Summit Trail	Moderate	1,000 feet	2.5 miles
West Slope Trail	Moderate	600 feet	3.9 miles
North Boundary Trail	Moderate	650 feet	2.8 miles
Quarry Road Trail	----	----	hikers only
South Summit Trail	Moderate	1,000 feet	2.1 miles
Bridge Bowl Trail	----	----	hikers only

Mt. Pisgah Trails (continued)

Some Mt. Pisgah trails run through oak, maple, and Douglas-fir forest.

Della, Van, and Dancer cruise along a trail on the side of Mt. Pisgah.

Mt. Pisgah

Highlights: If you want to see the entire south end of the Willamette Valley in a 360-degree panorama, or if you want to ride a variety of trails with good conditioning opportunities for your horse, then Mt. Pisgah is the place for you. The trails cross grassy meadows and go through dense, shady groves of oaks, maples, and Douglas-fir as they climb the steep slopes of Mt. Pisgah. The expansive views from the summit extend from the peaks of the Cascades to the Coast Range.

The Ride: The low-elevation Arboretum trails are for hikers only, but horses are welcome on the rest of the park's extensive network of trails. There is considerable elevation gain on the trails that go to the summit (over 1,000 feet of elevation change in 2.25 miles from the Frank Parrish Road parking lot), while the other trails climb more gradually. You can create your own loops on this extensive network of trails. Watch out for poison oak, as it is quite prevalent here. And try to stay on the park's official trails, because the user-created trails are not maintained and can be difficult.

*A shady grove gives Della, Van, and Dancer
a chance to cool off on a warm summer day.*

A canter is the cure for every evil.

Benjamin Disraeli
The Young Duke

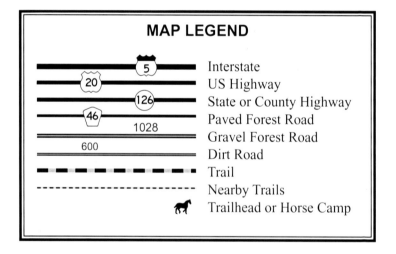

Nehalem Bay State Park

Northern Coastal Beaches

Oregon's northern coast offers plenty of opportunities for great horseback riding. Some of the area's horse-accessible beaches are on spits of land between the ocean and a bay, so at these locations you can choose a beach ride, a dune ride, a bay ride, or create a loop that includes all three.

Nehalem Bay State Park has an excellent horse camp, and you can ride to the beach from your campsite. Or you can rent a house with horse stalls only a short distance from Bayocean Peninsula. Nehalem Bay, Bayocean Peninsula, Sand Lake, and Bob Straub State Park are close enough to one another that no matter where you stay in the area, you can easily trailer to a different beach for a day ride.

Debbie on Mel and Whitney on Dixie, enjoying a beautiful day at Nehalem Bay State Park.

Northern Coast Beach Rides

Nehalem Bay State Park (above); the dunes on the bay side of Bob Straub State Park (right)

A beach ride at sunset (left); Bayocean Peninsula (below)

Getting to Nehalem Bay State Park

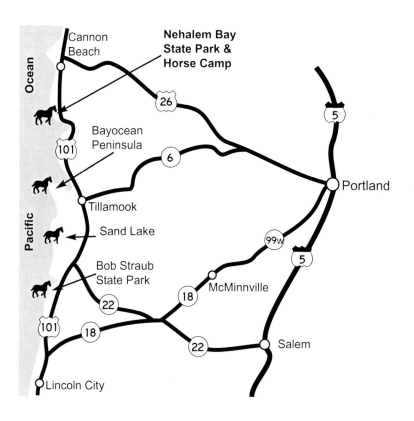

Northern Coast Area Trails

Trail	Difficulty	Elevation	Round Trip
Bayocean Peninsula	Easy	Sea level	Varies
Bob Straub State Park	Easy	Sea level	Varies
Nehalem Bay State Park	Easy	Sea level	Varies
Sand Lake	Easy	Sea level	Varies

Nehalem Bay State Park Horse Camp

Directions: Located 27 miles north of Tillamook and 15 miles south of Cannon Beach, off Highway 101. At the sign for Nehalem Bay State Park, turn south off Highway 101 and drive 1.3 miles to the park entrance. Continue 0.5 mile, turn left toward the campgrounds and continue 0.9 mile to the horse camp. If going to the day use parking area, don't turn off to the campground, but continue straight 1.0 mile farther.

Elevation: Sea level

Campsites: 17 sites, each with a 2-horse corral

Facilities: Portable toilets, drinking water, fire rings, picnic tables. Typically room for 1 rig per campsite. Most are back-in sites, but some are pull-through. Hot showers and flush toilets at the nearby people campground.

Permits: Fee campground

Season: Year-round

Trails: Ride at Nehalem Bay directly from the horse camp, or trailer to Bob Straub State Park, Sand Lake, or Bayocean Peninsula

Contact: Oregon State Parks, 800-452-5687, www.oregonstateparks.org/park_201.php

Campsites at Nehalem Bay Horse Camp are nestled among the coastal pines.

BayOcean House

Directions: Located overlooking Tillamook Bay, 4 miles northwest of Tillamook

Elevation: Sea level

Facilities: With 4 bedrooms, 3 bathrooms, futons, and hide-a-bed couches, this house on the shore of Tillamook Bay can sleep up to 15 people. Large kitchen, living room, family room, jacuzzi tub, hot tub, microwave, dishwasher, gas barbeque, deck. Four covered stalls for the horses. Big yard for parking trailers.

Cost: Varies by number of guests and time of year

Contact: www.bayocean.com, or call 503-657-0405

Trails: Bayocean Peninsula is a quick 2-mile trailer ride away, and Nehalem Bay, Sand Lake, and Bob Straub State Park are all within easy driving distance.

There's plenty of trailer parking at Bayocean House, located on the shore of scenic Tillamook Bay.

Bayocean Peninsula

Trailhead: Start at the Bayocean Peninsula parking area, 7 miles northwest of Tillamook
Length: Approximately 8.5 mile loop around the peninsula. Other rides are possible along the beach and through the dunes.
Elevation: Sea level
Difficulty: Easy
Season: Year round
Permits: None
Facilities: No facilities, no water. Parking for several trailers at the parking area.

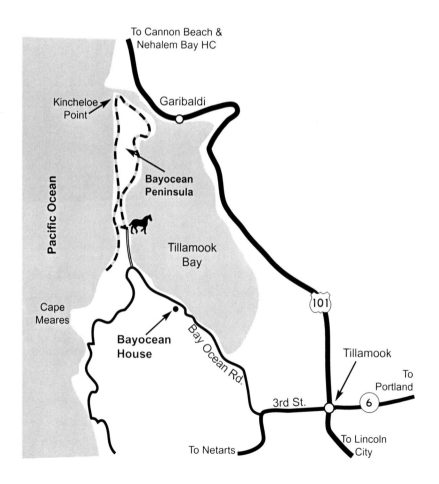

Debbie on Mel, Connie on Diamond, and Whitney on Dixie, exploring the Bayocean Peninsula at low tide.

Highlights: You can make a nice loop around the peninsula by riding north on the beach to Kincheloe Point, along the channel leading into Tillamook Bay, and back on the gravel road that runs along the bay. This area is very popular with the locals, and it's no wonder -- it's a terrific place to ride.

Finding the Trailhead: *From Nehalem Bay State Park*, go south 26 miles on Highway 101 to Tillamook. *From Tillamook*, drive west on 3rd Street. (If coming from the south, you'll have to turn west on 2nd St. or 4th St. and go around the block to reach 3rd St., because 3rd St. is one way going east for the first block.) Drive west on 3rd St. for 1.8 miles, turn right on Bay Ocean Road (toward Cape Meares) and continue 5.0 miles. Turn right on the graveled dike road and drive 0.9 mile to the large gravel parking area at the end of the road.

The Ride: The trail to the beach departs from the north end of the parking area. You can cross the dunes and ride along the 5-mile long expanse of beach, or make a loop by heading north on the beach for 3.5 miles, riding along the Tillamook Bay channel, and returning on the 3.6-mile gravel road that runs back to the parking area. For additional variety you can explore the dunes and the large tree-covered knoll near the north end of the peninsula using the network of trails that runs through them.

Bob Straub State Park

Trailhead: Start at the boat ramp parking area at Bob Straub State Park in Pacific City, 28 miles south of Tillamook and 21 miles north of Lincoln City
Length: Round trip around the spit is about 7.5 miles, and there are multiple additional trails through the dunes
Elevation: Sea level
Difficulty: Easy
Season: Year round
Permits: None
Facilities: Restrooms, no water. Parking for many trailers in the boat ramp parking lot.

Highlights: Dunes covered with coastal pines provide an interesting start to this ride, after which you'll come out on the beautiful Nes-

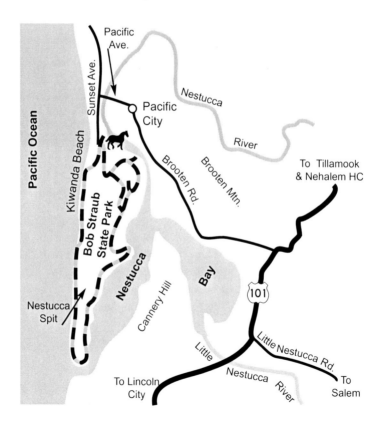

tucca spit. You can make a loop around the spit, or choose among the many trails through the dunes to create your own route.

Finding the Trailhead: *From Tillamook*, drive south 25 miles on Highway 101. *From Nehalem Bay State Park*, go south 45 miles on Highway 101. *From Lincoln City*, drive north 18 miles on Highway 101. Turn west on Brooten Rd. toward Pacific City. Drive about 3 miles to the town of Pacific City and turn west on Pacific Avenue. Continue 0.2 mile and turn left on Sunset Avenue, the first street after you cross the Nestucca River. Drive 0.4 mile and turn left into the park's parking and boat-launching area.

The Ride: Pick up the trail on the south edge of the parking lot. The first part of the trail runs through the dunes and among the coastal pines, and there are many trails through this area. Keep veering to the left if you want to reach the bay or right if you want to go to the beach, and you'll eventually make your way there. Watch for seals and sea lions playing in the bay or sunning themselves along the bay shore.

Julie, Debbie, and Dennis ride along the bay side of Nestucca Spit at Bob Straub State Park.

Nehalem Bay State Park

Trailhead: Start at Nehalem Bay State Park campground or day parking area
Length: Varies. The beach is 4 miles long, or you can ride through the dunes and for a short distance along the bay.
Elevation: Sea level
Difficulty: Easy
Season: Year round
Permits: Fee to camp or park
Facilities: Toilets, drinking water, easy parking for several trailers in the day-use area

Highlights: Is there anything more exhilarating than riding your horse down a beautiful beach, with the surf pounding and the sand stretch-

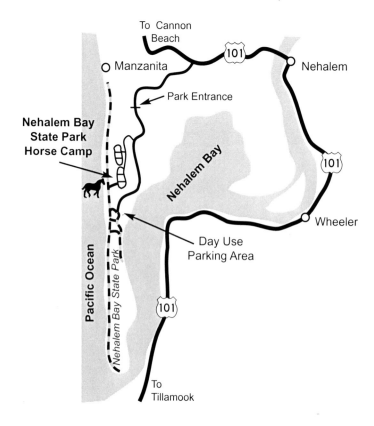

*Connie and Diamond enjoy a breezy walk
down the beach at Nehalem Bay State Park.*

ing away for miles before you? If you love this kind of riding (and who doesn't?) then Nehalem Bay State Park is the place for you.

Finding the Trailhead: Take Highway 101 north *from Tillamook* about 27 miles, or go south on Highway 101 *from Cannon Beach* about 15 miles. At the sign for Nehalem Bay State Park, turn south and drive 1.3 miles through a residential area to the park entrance. Continue 0.5 mile, turn left toward the campgrounds and drive 0.9 mile to the horse camp. If going to the day use parking area, don't turn off to the campground, but continue straight 1.0 mile more.

The Ride: You can ride to the beach from either the campground or the day parking area by heading west on one of the trails through the dunes. Or you can head east to reach a trail that runs a short distance along the bay side (it dead-ends after about 0.7 mile). The 4-mile long beach is beautiful, and offers a wonderful riding experience.

Sand Lake

Trailhead: Start from the day-use parking area at the Sand Beach campground, 18 miles south of Tillamook or 38 miles north of Lincoln City
Length: Varies
Elevation: Sea level
Difficulty: Easy
Season: Year round
Permits: None
Facilities: Toilets and parking for several trailers in the day-use area

Highlights: Sand Lake is a very popular destination for ATV riders because of the nearby dunes. But if you ride on a weekday (especially in fall and winter) you should have the place pretty much to yourself.

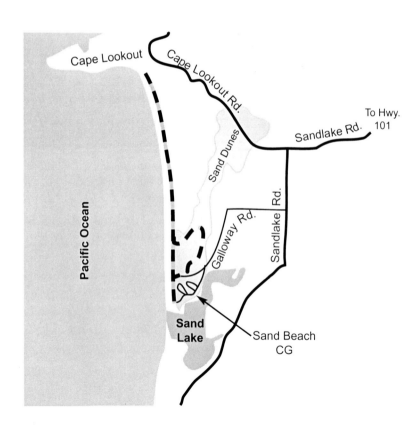

The 4.5-mile long beach is lovely, and the huge expanse of sand dunes offers a unique riding experience.

Finding the Trailhead: *From Tillamook*, drive south on Highway 101 for 10 miles. *From Nehalem Bay State Park*, go south on Highway 101 for 37 miles. *From Lincoln City*, drive north on Hwy. 101 for 30 miles. Turn west on Sandlake Road and continue 5.5 miles. Turn right on Galloway Road and drive 2.6 miles, then turn left into Sand Beach campground. Continue 0.3 mile to the Fisherman day-use area.

The Ride: Begin by riding along the shore of Sand Lake toward the ocean. The dunes will be on your right and Sand Lake on your left. You can ride along the beach all the way to Cape Lookout, or detour up the hillside and onto the dunes.

Sandy, Kelly, Debbie (with Baby Rylee), and Deb on the dunes at Sand Lake. Cape Lookout is in the background.

There are good views from the dunes near Sand Lake. The dunes are shared with ATVs.

We gaze upon their quiet beauty, their natural elegance, and we are captivated. They see us softly, in gentle light . . . rewarding human companionship with strength, grace, and intelligence. As they run through arenas and open fields, past mountains and seas, moving like the wind toward heaven, we travel with them, if only in our hearts.

Anonymous

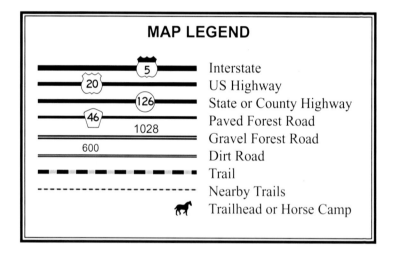

Northrup Creek Horse Camp

Clatsop State Forest

Nestled next to Northrup Creek in the Coast Range about 70 miles west of Portland, 35 miles southeast of Astoria, and 25 miles southwest of Clatskanie, Northrup Creek horse camp offers some very nice forest riding. The horse camp opened in 2005, and as of this writing there is only one designated horse trail near the camp. But more trails are planned for the future and there are plenty of nearby forest roads to explore in the meantime.

Like much of the coast range, the Northrup Creek area features lush vegetation, towering trees, and plenty of wildflowers in season. Because of its inland location, Northrup Creek horse camp can often be sunny even when the weather on the coast is gray.

Foxglove blooming beside the Northrup Creek Loop.

Northrup Creek Horse Camp

Directions: *From Portland:* From the junction of Hwy. 26 (Sunset Hwy.) and Hwy. 217, take Hwy. 26 west for 47.5 miles, go north on Hwy. 103 toward Jewell for 9 miles, drive east on Hwy. 202 for 6 miles, and then at milepost 35 go north 4 miles on Northrup Creek Rd.
From Astoria: Drive 35 miles southeast on Hwy. 202, then at milepost 35 go north 4 miles on Northrup Creek Road.
From Seaside: Drive south on Hwy. 101 to Hwy. 26, then go east 21.5 miles. Turn north on Hwy. 103 toward Jewell and go 9 miles, turn east on Hwy. 202 and drive 6 miles, and then at milepost 35 go north 4 miles on Northrup Creek Rd.

Elevation: 700 feet

Campsites: 8 campsites with 4-horse log corrals that are built to accommodate tarp covers. 3 sites for non-equestrian use.

Facilities: Vault toilet, hand-pumped potable water, manure bins. Two pull-through sites offer parking for 2 trailers, and the remainder are back-in sites with room for 1 trailer. Firewood available for purchase May through September. The day-use area has parking for several rigs and offers a toilet and picnic tables.

Permits: User fee, or Northwest Forest Pass required for day use parking.

Season: April thru November

Contact: Clatsop State Forest, 503-359-5435, www.oregon.gov/odf/field/astoria/state_forest_management/recreation_main.shtml#campgrounds

Northrup Creek Area Trails

Trail	Difficulty	Elevation	Round Trip
Northrup Creek Loop	Moderate	550-1,200	8.5 miles

Getting to Northrup Creek

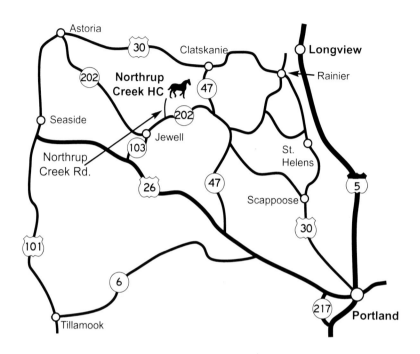

The vegetation at Northrup Creek Horse Camp is lush and green.

Northrup Creek Loop

Trailhead: Start at Northrup Creek Horse Camp
Length: 8.5 miles
Elevation: 550 to 1,200 feet
Difficulty: Moderate, though the trail can be slippery after a rain
Season: Spring through fall
Permits: User fee for horse camp. NW Forest Pass required for day use parking.
Facilities: Toilet and potable water at the horse camp. Stock water is available on the trail.

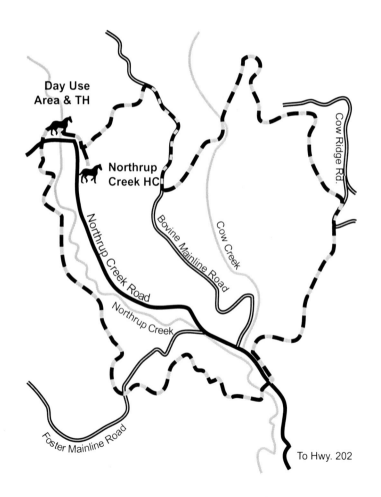

Lydia on Shadow and Connie on Diamond, enjoying one of the forest-road segments of Northrup Creek Loop.

Highlights: This pleasant loop trail runs partially on single-track trails and partially on forest roads. With the exception of a couple of clearcut areas, the trail runs through dense moss-draped forests. In places the shade is so deep that there is little undergrowth, but in most places the vegetation is lush. The wildflowers are a delight.

The Ride: The trail departs from either the day-use area or the north side of the campground, between sites 2 and 3. It goes over ridges and along the bank of Northrup Creek, then back through the day-use area. It is well marked and easy to follow. As of 2008, most of the trail is single track, but some of the segments are on forest roads. Note that if it has been raining heavily the trail can become muddy and slick, so if the weather is wet the local forest roads may be a better choice. We understand that additional trails are planned for the future, so you can try out the camp now and come back again in a year or two to see what has changed.

While there are many things you can fake through in this life, pretending that you know horses when you don't isn't one of them.

Cooky McClung
Horsefolk are Different

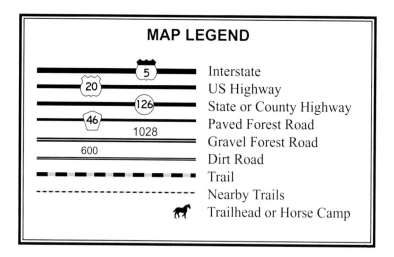

Reehers Camp

Tillamook State Forest

Reehers Camp is located 42 miles west of Portland and 48 miles east of Tillamook, so riders in the Hillsboro/Forest Grove area enjoy a nice horse camp very close to home. The Gales Creek Trail was the camp's only trail when we were there in 2007, and it's a good one. It takes you up to the summit of Round Top Mountain, then down the other side along the lovely Gales Creek to the Storey Burn trailhead, and beyond if you are so inclined. Several logging roads near camp create additional riding opportunities. Two additional trails are expected to be completed in 2009: the Step Creek Trail, which will connect to the Gales Creek Trail at two points to create a 5-mile loop, and a second loop trail on the north side of Cochran Road, near the Nehalem River bridge. Details on the two new trails were not available when this book went to press, but you can check the Tillamook State Forest website for the latest information.

The horse camp opened in 2005 and is located on the site of a historic Civilian Conservation Corp camp of the 1930's and early 1940's. It is shaded by huge fir, alder, and maple trees, and features a hand pump with potable water, a camp host, and a large group shelter. There is also a large day-use area that has picnic tables, a toilet, and room to park 4 to 6 trailers.

The group picnic shelter at Reehers Camp.

Reehers Camp

Directions: *From Portland:* From the junction of Hwy. 26 and Hwy. 217, go west on Hwy. 26 for 32 miles, turn south on Timber Rd. and continue 3 miles to the town of Timber. Turn west on Cochran Rd. and drive 2.5 miles to Reehers Camp. *From Tillamook:* Drive east on Hwy. 6 for 39 miles, turn north on Timber Rd and go 6 miles to the town of Timber. Turn west on Cochran Rd. and continue 2.5 miles to Reehers Camp.

Elevation: 1,100 feet

Campsites: 10 sites with log corrals for 4 horses each, plus 6 non-equestrian sites. One site is a pull-thru that can accept 2 trailers. The rest are back-in sites for one vehicle.

Facilities: Toilet, stock water, camp host, group shelter, manure bins, and trash/recycling bins. All corrals have high center beams to suspend tarps over. Firewood available for purchase.

Permits: User fee for camp

Season: May through October

Contact: Tillamook State Forest, 503-359-7401, www.oregon.gov/odf/tsf/reehers.shtml

Reehers Camp Area Trails

Trail	Difficulty	Elevation	Round Trip
Gales Creek trail from Reehers to summit	Moderate	1,100-2,600	7 miles
Gales Creek trail from Storey Burn TH to summit	Moderate	1,800-2,600	11 miles
Gales Creek trail from Reehers to Storey Burn trailhead	Moderate	1,100-2,600	18 miles

Getting to Reehers Camp

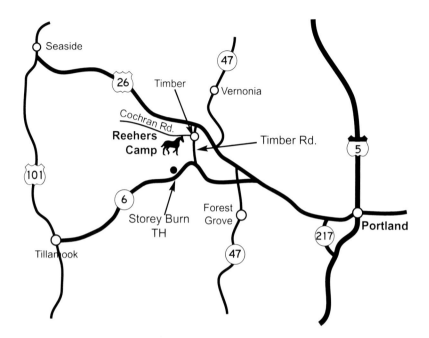

Tex, Shadow, and Diamond lounge around at Reehers Camp.

Gales Creek Trail

Trailhead: Start at Reehers Camp, or at the Storey Burn trailhead off Hwy. 6

Length: 18 miles round trip from Reehers Camp to the Storey Burn trailhead, or 7 miles round trip from Reehers Camp to the summit of Roundtop Mtn., or 11 miles round trip from Storey Burn trailhead to the summit

Elevation: 1,100 to 2,600 feet from either Reehers Camp or Storey Burn trailhead to the summit

Difficulty: Moderate, but the trail can become slippery after rain

Season: Late spring through fall

Permits: User fee for horse camp

Facilities: Toilet and stock water at the horse camp. Stock water is available on the trail.

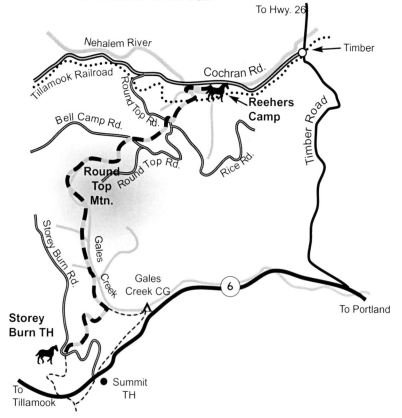

Connie on Diamond and Lydia on Shadow sauntering along the Gales Creek trail after a rainstorm.

Highlights: The Gales Creek Trail climbs from Reehers Camp to near the summit of Round Top Mountain, then descends to Storey Burn trailhead along the bank of the lovely Gales Creek. It is a nice forest ride that offers great views of Mt. Hood, Mt. St. Helens, and Mt. Adams from the top of Round Top Mountain on a clear day.

The Ride: The trail departs from the day-use area at Reehers Camp and after an easy first mile it climbs steadily, crossing several logging roads and the Tillamook Railroad track. After 3.5 miles (and 1,500 feet of elevation gain) you'll cross the shoulder of Round Top Mountain and be rewarded with spectacular views of the nearby Cascade peaks. The trail then drops into a gorge created by Gales Creek, and for some of its length it follows an overgrown road used to clear salvage timber after the Tillamook Burn. The stretch along Gales Creek is the prettiest part of the trail, and it can be accessed from the Storey Burn trailhead (off Highway 6) if you want to see this segment but don't want to ride the entire 18-mile round trip.

When you're young and you fall off a horse, you may break something. When you're my age and you fall off, you splatter.

Roy Rogers

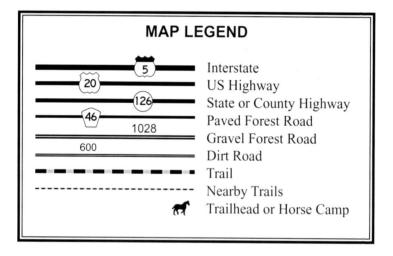

Sam Brown Horse Camp

Siskiyou National Forest

Located 29 miles west of Grants Pass, Sam Brown Horse Camp is nestled in a beautiful valley between steep tree-covered ridges. Several good trails are accessible from the camp, ranging from the easy Onion Way Trail to the moderate Briggs Creek and Taylor Creek Trails and the more difficult Dutchy Creek Trail. The Secret Way Trail, which climbs over Secret Ridge, is also nearby but we didn't ride it because it was blocked by fallen trees. There are interesting old mining sites in the area, and several creeks are near the trails. Wildflowers bloom profusely in season.

Sam Brown is a wonderful horse camp. Each site has a fire pit, picnic table, and corrals, and the camp has potable water, a toilet, a nice meadow, and the lovely Myers Creek flowing along its south edge.

Wild iris blooms along the perimeter of the campground.

Sam Brown Horse Camp

Directions: Located 29 miles west of Grants Pass. Take I-5 north from Grants Pass 3 miles to the Merlin exit (exit 61) and turn west on the Merlin-Galice Rd. toward the town of Merlin. Continue for 12.2 miles and turn left on Taylor Creek Road (Road 25). This paved one-lane road (with occasional turnouts for downhill traffic) winds steeply up over Lone Tree Pass and down into Briggs Valley. After 13.5 miles, turn right on Road 2512 and cross the bridge to the horse camp.

Elevation: 2,000 feet

Campsites: 7 campsites with log corrals for 2 or 4 horses each

Facilities: Toilet, potable water. Parking for 1 trailer per campsite.

Permits: User fee, or Northwest Forest Pass required for day-use parking

Season: Late spring through fall

Contact: Galice Ranger District, 541-471-6500, www.fs.fed.us/r6/rogue-siskiyou/recreation/camping/ index.html

Mel and Jane enjoy their breakfast at Sam Brown Horse Camp.

Getting to Sam Brown Horse Camp

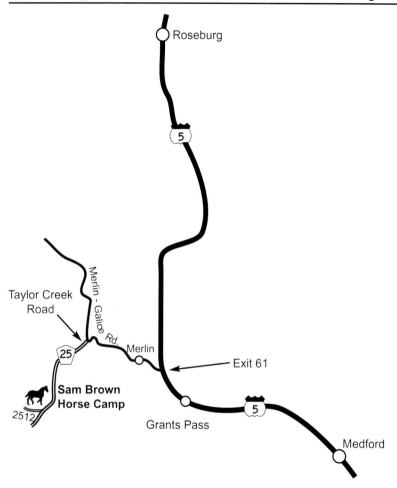

Sam Brown Area Trails

Trail	Difficulty	Elevation	Round Trip
Briggs Creek Trail	Moderate	1,600-2,200	5 or 9 miles
Dutchy Creek Trail	Challenging	2,000-3,500	6 or 12 miles
Onion Way Trail	Easy	2,000-2,300	5 miles
Taylor Creek Trail	Moderate	2,000-2,700	9+ miles

Briggs Creek Trail

Trailhead: Start at Sam Brown Horse Camp
Length: 5 miles round trip to Elkhorn Mine, or 9 miles round trip to Courier Mine
Elevation: 1,600 to 2,200 feet
Difficulty: Moderate
Season: Late spring through fall
Permits: User fee for horse camp
Facilities: Toilet and potable water at the horse camp. Stock water is available on the trail.

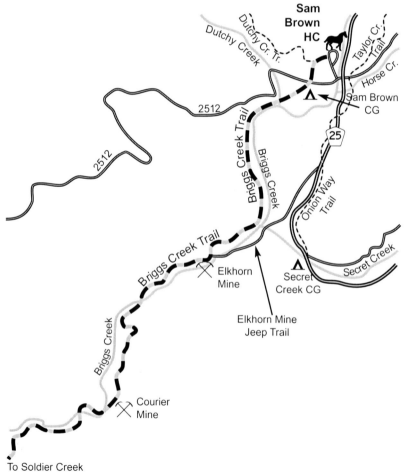

Debbie and Mel enjoy the cool shade of a creek crossing.

Highlights: This is a very pleasant forested trail that follows Briggs Creek. There are several creek crossings, and on a hot day the creek offers some good swimming holes. The trail runs past a couple of interesting old mining sites. Unfortunately, when we rode this trail in June 2007 fallen trees across the trail prevented us from reaching either Elkhorn Mine or Courier Mine.

The Ride: The trail departs near the fee station at Sam Brown Horse Camp and goes through lovely forested terrain. After 0.4 mile, the trail to Dutchy Creek splits off to the right. Veer left and continue another 0.3 mile to Road 2512 and the entrance to Sam Brown Campground. Cross Road 2512 and pick up the dirt road on the right just before the entrance to the campground. The double-track road soon becomes a trail, crosses several creeks, and after about 2 miles it reaches the site of the old Elkhorn Mine. About 2 miles later it passes the historic Courier Mine. If desired, you can continue several more miles to an old camp near Soldier Creek and Road 4305, where the trail ends.

Dutchy Creek Trail

Trailhead: Start at Sam Brown Horse Camp
Length: 6 miles round trip to summit only, or 12 miles round trip for loop using Road 2402 and Road 2512
Elevation: 2,000 to 3,500 feet
Difficulty: Challenging: narrow trail traverses very steep hillsides, steep and rocky toward the top of the ridge
Season: Late spring through fall
Permits: User fee
Facilities: Toilet and potable water at the horse camp. No water on the trail.

Highlights: The Dutchy Creek Trail is a steady climb on a narrow trail that traverses the side of a very steep ridge. Toward the top of the

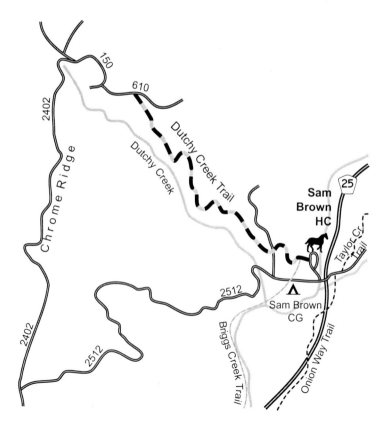

ridge, the trail becomes steep and rocky and there is little shade. The forest on the way up is pretty, ranging from stands of Douglas-fir to live oak and madrone. There are awe-inspiring views from near the top of the ridge.

The Ride: The trail begins near the fee station at Sam Brown horse camp. About 0.4 mile from the trailhead, the Briggs Creek Trail goes to the left. Veer right on the Dutchy Creek Trail (toward Silver Creek, according to the sign). After another 0.4 mile, the trail crosses a dirt road. From there the trail climbs steadily, traversing the steep slope carved by Dutchy Creek far below. About 2.3 miles from the trailhead the forest gives way to manzanita bushes and the trail gets steeper and fairly rocky. At the top there are striking views of the Briggs Valley and surrounding ridges.

To make a loop, go left on Road 610 for 0.4 mile, then veer right on Road 150. In another 0.5 mile, turn left on Road 2402 and traverse Chrome Ridge for 3.6 miles. Turn left on Road 2512 and follow it 5.0 miles back to the horse camp.

Debbie and Mel admire the vistas from near the top of Chrome Ridge.

Onion Way Trail

Trailhead: Start at Sam Brown Horse Camp
Length: 5 miles round trip
Elevation: 2,000 to 2,300 feet
Difficulty: Easy
Season: Late spring through fall
Permits: User fee for horse camp
Facilities: Toilet and potable water at the horse camp. Stock water is available on the trail.

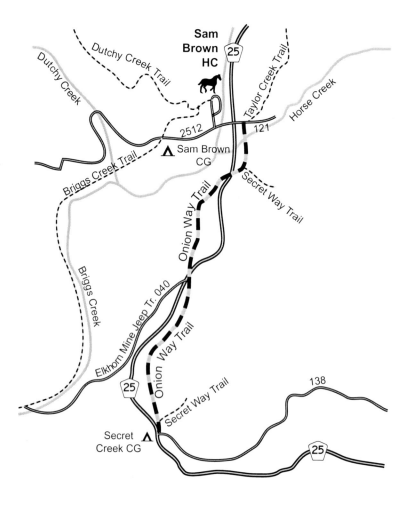

Highlights: The Onion Way Trail was used in the early 1900s to reach the mines on Onion Creek from the Sam Brown area. It runs through lush forest and pretty meadows that offer abundant wildflowers in season. Most of the trail is densely shaded. This is an easy trail that is a good arrival-day warm-up ride for the longer trails nearby.

The Ride: Follow the road out of the horse camp to Road 2512, turn left and cross Road 25, then travel a short distance down Road 121. The Onion Way trailhead is on the right. The trail crosses Horse Creek and goes through lovely old-growth Douglas-fir forest and small meadows filled with wildflowers in season. About 0.4 mile from the trailhead, the trail crosses Road 25, and after another 0.6 mile it crosses it again. About 1.1 miles beyond this, the trail ends at Secret Creek campground.

You can access the Secret Way Trail from the Onion Way Trail either 0.3 mile from the trailhead or about 0.2 mile from the Secret Creek campground. However, we couldn't ride it because it was blocked by fallen trees. We understand that the Secret Way Trail is a strenuous loop that offers nice views from the top of the ridge. BONUS: If you pick up the Elkhorn Mine jeep trail (Road 040) off Road 25, you can link to the Briggs Creek trail and create a 5-mile loop ride.

Debbie and Mel enter a sunny meadow along the Onion Way trail.

Taylor Creek Trail

Trailhead: Start at Sam Brown Horse Camp
Length: 9 miles round trip to Lone Tree Pass. Longer rides are possible.
Elevation: 2,000 to 2,700 feet
Difficulty: Moderate
Season: Late spring through fall
Permits: User fee for horse camp
Facilities: Toilet and potable water at the horse camp. The only water on this section of the trail is at Horse Creek, near the trailhead.

Highlights: The Taylor Creek Trail runs 10.25 miles (one way), with five trailheads along Road 25. We rode the segment closest to Sam Brown horse camp, which goes to Lone Tree Pass. This portion of the

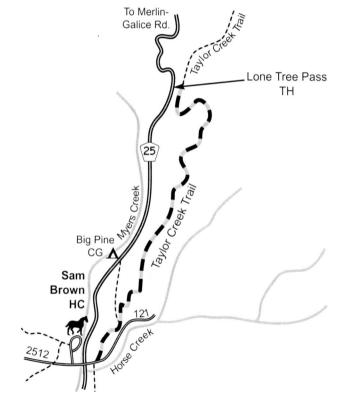

Debbie and Mel saunter up the Taylor Creek trail not far from Sam Brown Horse Camp.

trail goes through dense Douglas-fir forest, through stands of live oak and madrone, and through a couple of areas that were clear-cut several years ago and now feature dense brush, small trees, and occasional views of the surrounding ridges.

The Ride: Follow the road out of the horse camp to Road 2512, turn left and cross Road 25, and go a short distance down Road 121. The Taylor Creek Trail departs on the left. The initial stretch of the trail goes through forest so dense that most undergrowth has been shaded out. After 0.7 mile you'll reach a junction where a trail splits off on the left to Big Pine campground (1.25 miles away). Stay to the right. As the trail climbs the vegetation gives way to live oak and madrone, and for about 1.6 miles the trail runs along the east side of the ridge, just below the crest. Then it crosses to the west side of the ridge and continues along it 1.7 miles to Lone Tree Pass and a trailhead on Road 25. The trail continues another 6 or 7 miles northward through the deep valley carved by Taylor Creek. Besides the trailheads at Sam Brown (Briggs Valley) and Lone Tree Pass, the Taylor Creek Trail has four other trailheads along Road 25. Several of these are large enough to accommodate a horse trailer, so you can trailer out and explore a different section of the trail if you would like.

To be loved by a horse, or by any animal, should fill us with awe—for we have not deserved it.

Marion Garretty

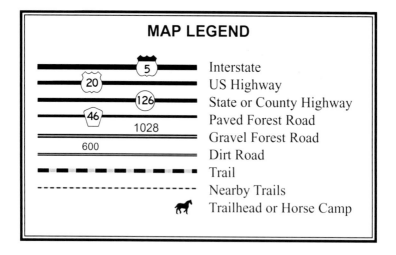

Santiam Horse Camp

Santiam State Forest

Thirty miles east of Salem is an undiscovered gem of a horse camp. Situated in the Santiam State Forest outside the town of Gates, Santiam Horse Camp is a 9-site campground with plenty of amenities and some really nice trails to ride. Best of all, the trails are a work in progress, so you can ride them now and come back next year to see how the trail system has been enlarged and enhanced. At the time this chapter was written (summer 2008), there was an 8-mile loop trail out of camp, plus a mini-loop that you can take your non-horsey friends on without overwhelming them. Additional trails are in the works that will create several more loop opportunities. Stay tuned!

Cindy on Cairo, ZoAnne on Sonata, and Tina on Indy, having a great time on the Monument Peak Loop.

Santiam Horse Camp

Directions: From Salem, take Highway 22 east for 30 miles to the town of Gates. Turn south on Horeb Road, and in 0.1 mile turn left on Sorbin Street. Continue through Gates for 0.3 mile and turn right on Gates School Road. Go 1.1 mile and turn left on Henness Lane. Where this road turns to gravel it becomes Monument Peak Road. Continue 1.1 mile and turn right on Christmas Tree Road, then drive 0.5 mile to the campground.

Elevation: 1,700 feet

Campsites: 9 sites with log corrals for 4 horses each. Eight sites are back-ins with room for one trailer, and one site is a pull-through with room for two vehicles.

Facilities: Toilet, stock water, no drinking water. Group shelter. Picnic tables, fire pits, hitching rails, camp host, manure bins, firewood for sale. Parking for many rigs at both the horse camp day-use area and the lower Monument Peak Road day-use area.

Permits: User fee for camp

Season: May 1 - October 31

Contact: www.oregon.gov/ODF/field/north_cascade/aboutus.html or 503-859-2151

Moose and Diamond chow down in the corrals at Santiam Horse Camp.

Getting to Santiam Horse Camp

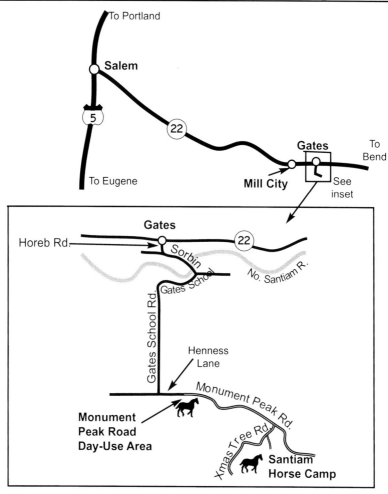

Santiam Horse Camp Area Trails

Trail	Difficulty	Elevation	Round Trip
Mad Creek Canyon Loop	Moderate	1,300-2,600	9 miles
Turnidge Creek Loop	Easy	1,650-1,900	1.5 miles

Mad Creek Canyon Loop

Trailhead: Start at Santiam Horse Camp or at the Monument Peak Road Day-use Staging Area

Length: 9 miles round trip from Santiam Horse Camp; 11 miles round trip from the Monument Peak day-use area

Elevation: 1,300 to 2,600 feet from the horse camp, or 1,100 to 2,600 feet from the Monument Peak day-use area

Difficulty: Moderate. Some muddy spots in season. Forest roads are rocky, which may be tough on barefoot horses.

Season: Late spring through fall

Permits: User fee for horse camp

Facilities: Toilets, stock water, hitching rails, picnic table, manure bins in camp. Stock water is available on the trail.

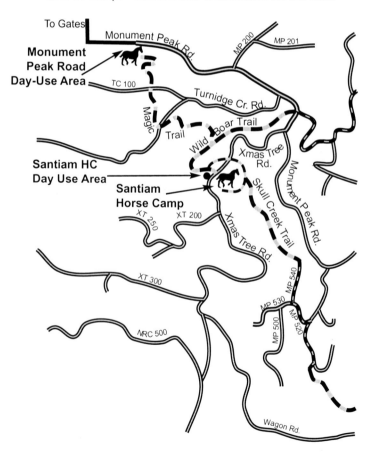

Highlights: This delightful trail runs on single-track trails and forest roads, traveling through dense forest as well as areas that have been clear-cut. The result is a lot of variety in what you'll see along the trail. All trail junctions are clearly marked. And the best part is that the trail is a work in progress -- additional trails are in the works that will enlarge the trail network and make it possible to ride several alternative loops. In addition, the Santiam State Forest plans to replace the forest-road segments with single-track segments in the future. On a hot summer day we enjoyed riding the loop in a clockwise direction (starting out on the Wild Boar Trail), because this allowed us to cover most of the sunny sections of the trail in the morning, leaving the shady sections for later in the day.

The Ride: To ride the loop clockwise, depart from the trailhead in the day-use parking area across Christmas Tree Road from the entrance to the horse camp. After a short distance you'll come to a trail junction.

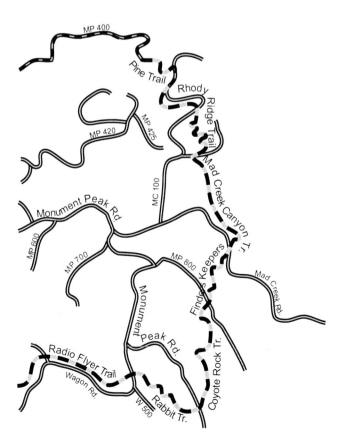

Mad Creek Canyon Loop (cont.)

Turn left toward the Wild Boar Trail. This segment of the trail features dense shade and for some of its length you'll be riding on an old railroad grade. About 0.65 mile from camp the Magic Trail to the lower day use area goes off to the left. Stay on the Wild Boar Trail, cross Monument Peak Road, and continue on Road 400 for 1.6 miles, then pick up the Pine Trail. When the trail reaches a gravel road, turn right and follow it a short distance, then pick up the Rhody Ridge Trail on the right. It runs through a clear-cut area and offers good views of the surrounding hills and the valley below. When the trail crosses another gravel road it becomes the Mad Creek Canyon Trail, which runs through a deep ravine carved by Mad Creek. In winter you can see a waterfall across the canyon. In summer the thick foliage hides the waterfall, but you'll still be able to hear it. Then the trail crosses Mad Creek Road and becomes the Finders Keepers Trail, which runs through dense forest. When the trail crosses Road 800 it becomes the Coyote Rock Trail. Watch for the actual Coyote Rock, uphill from the trail. Then the trail crosses Monument Peak Road and it becomes the Rabbit Trail. And after crossing Wagon Road it turns into the Radio Flyer Trail. This eventually comes out on a gravel road. Go left and

Connie is riding Diamond, Ray is on Moose, and Whitney is riding Dixie on a sunny section of Road 520.

in a short distance turn left again on Road 520 and then right on Road 540. This runs into the Skull Creek Trail, which will take you back to camp. To ride the trail counter-clockwise, take the perimeter trail that circles the horse camp, and between campsites 2 and 3 you'll see the beginning of the Skull Creek Trail.

Tina on Indy and ZoAnne on Sonata as they move out on the trail.

Connie on Diamond, Whitney on Dixie, and Ray on Moose, riding the Rhody Ridge section of the Monument Peak Loop.

Turnidge Creek Loop

Trailhead: Start at Santiam Horse Camp
Length: 1.5 miles round trip
Elevation: 1,650 to 1,950 feet
Difficulty: Easy
Season: Late spring through fall
Permits: User fee for horse camp
Facilities: Toilets, stock water, hitching rails, picnic tables, fire pits, manure pits in camp. No water on the trail.

Highlights: This ride will seem absurdly short to real riders -- hardly worth saddling up for. Locals have dubbed this trail "Spouse Loop" because if you take a non-rider spouse or friend along, they'll be bowled over by the spectacular trees you show them and will think the

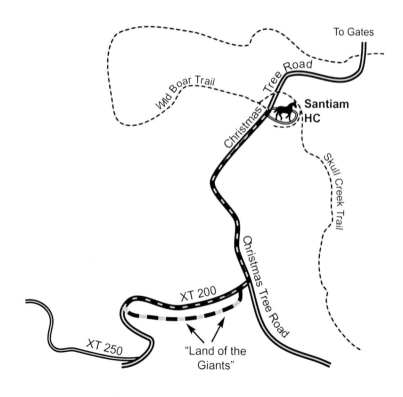

ride length is just right. And they'll want to go "riding" with you again in the future!

The Ride: This trail will eventually be extended to connect to the Wild Boar Trail. For now, though, from the entrance to Santiam Horse Camp you'll turn left and ride along Christmas Tree Road. After about 0.6 mile, veer right on Road 200 (the first gravel road you come to), and almost immediately pick up the single track trail that departs on your left. This trail will lead you along a hillside and past some of the largest old-growth Douglas-fir trees you've ever laid eyes on. The trail truly runs through "The Land of the Giants", and is a grand way to introduce your non-riding buddies to the wonderful sights we get to see when we ride. After 0.5 mile, the single-track trail rejoins Road 200. Turn right and ride Road 200 and Christmas Tree Road back to camp, or turn around and retrace your route through the old-growth timber and back to the horse camp. Your horses won't be sweaty, and your friends will be awed.

*This trail runs through The Land of the Giants
-- giant trees, that is.*

There is something about riding down the street on a prancing horse that makes you feel like something even when you ain't a thing.

Will Rogers

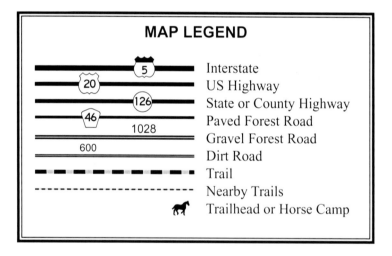

Sevenmile Horse Camp

Willamette National Forest

Sevenmile Horse Camp is located east of Corvallis and Sweet Home, off Highway 20 near Tombstone Pass. It offers good riding with a historical twist: access to a 20-mile stretch of the Old Santiam Wagon Road. This historic wagon road was built in the 1860's and became a critical route for transporting livestock and freight between the Willamette Valley and Central Oregon and westward to the gold mines in Idaho and eastern Oregon. Officially called the Willamette Valley and Cascade Mountain Road, it operated as a toll road until 1915, and in 1925 was turned over to the state of Oregon to become a highway. Today some segments of the Wagon Road have become obliterated, but the intact sections are connected by single-track trails so you can still ride the route of the old road and get a fascinating glimpse back into history.

The trails near Sevenmile Horse Camp mostly follow the historic route of the Old Santiam Wagon Road.

Sevenmile Horse Camp

Directions: From Sweet Home, drive east on Hwy. 20 for 32 miles. Just past milepost 59, turn south on Road 024 and continue 0.5 mile to the horse camp.

Elevation: 3,000 feet

Campsites: 4 sites with log corrals. One site has 4 stalls, 2 sites have 2 stalls, and one site has 3 stalls. All sites are back-in and fairly level, and two are large enough for two vehicles.

Facilities: Toilet, picnic tables, fire rings, hitching rails, manure bin, stock water. No drinking water. Large parking area can accommodate several day-use trailers.

Permits: Northwest Forest Pass required

Season: Summer through fall

Contact: www.fs.fed.us/r6/willamette/recreation/tripplanning/index.html or 541-367-5168

The two upper campsites at Sevenmile share five corrals.

Getting to Sevenmile Horse Camp

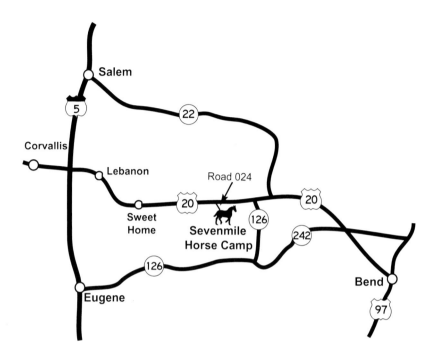

Sevenmile Area Trails

Trail	Difficulty	Elevation	Round Trip
Old Santiam Wagon Rd. E.	Moderate	2,900-4,250	10.5 miles
Old Santiam Wagon Rd. W.	Challenging	1,650-2,900	9.0 miles

Old Santiam Wagon Road East

Trailhead: Start at Sevenmile Horse Camp
Length: 10.5 miles round trip to Tombstone Pass
Elevation: 2,900 to 4,250 feet
Difficulty: Moderate: a short section near the summit traverses a steep side hill, one big creek crossing and several small ones.
Season: Summer through fall
Permits: Northwest Forest Pass required
Facilities: Toilets and stock water at the horse camp. Stock water is available on the trail.

Highlights: The Old Santiam Wagon Road climbs steadily through mostly second-growth forest to Tombstone Pass and continues beyond. On the way it crosses several trickling streams and the good-sized Snow Creek, and it provides glimpses of Jump-off Joe Mountain, Iron Mountain, and Green Mountain. In places you can hear Sevenmile Creek far below you as the trail hugs the upper flank of the mountain. While you ride along you realize how challenging it must have been to build the wagon road in the first place, and how much work it was for teams to pull fully-loaded wagons up these grades and brake them

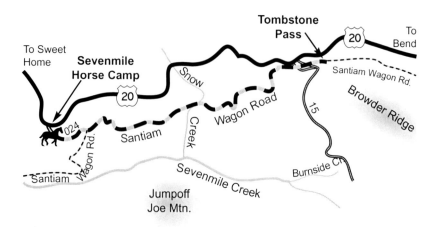

Connie on Diamond and Ray on Moose, enjoying the forest along the Old Santiam Wagon Road to the east of camp.

on the long downhill slopes. The first transcontinental auto race used the Santiam Wagon Road to cross the Cascades in 1905, and the cars had to tie logs behind them to slow their steep descent.

The Ride: The trail departs from the east side of the horse camp, following Road 024 for about 0.75 mile. Turn left on the clearly-marked single-track trail that leads toward Tombstone Pass. In places the trail follows the old wagon road, but in other areas it follows newer logging roads or becomes a single-track trail. You'll see areas where the old wagon road was seriously washed out by spring runoff, and in one spot you can see the remains of an old log bridge that collapsed into the stream below. In the winter of 2007/08 the relatively new bridge over Snow Creek collapsed because of the weight of the winter snows, so as of this writing you must ford the creek. This trail isn't as rocky or narrow as the one heading west from camp, but a portion of the last mile before Tombstone Pass is on a fairly steep side slope. Unfortunately, there are no real views from the top of Tombstone Pass, but along the way you'll get glimpses of the nearby mountaintops through the trees.

Old Santiam Wagon Road West

Trailhead: Start at Sevenmile Horse Camp
Length: 9 miles round trip to House Rock Campground
Elevation: 1,650-2,900 feet
Difficulty: Challenging: the trail traverses several steep hillsides on a narrow trail and is rocky in places (tough for barefoot horses). Some small creek crossings.
Season: Summer through fall
Permits: Northwest Forest Pass required
Facilities: Toilet and stock water at the horse camp. Stock water is available on the trail.

Highlights: This trail offers a real glimpse into Oregon's past as it follows the route of the Old Santiam Wagon Road. Some segments of the wagon road are no longer passable so in these sections the road becomes a single-track trail that leads to the next rideable section. These narrow trails traverse some steep hillsides that can be a bit

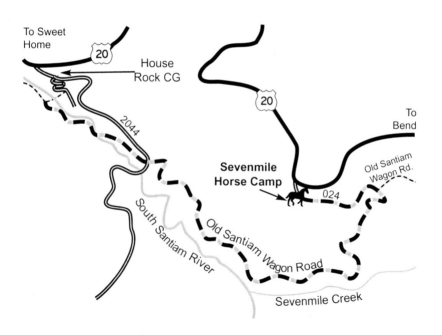

daunting if you don't like heights. However, the historical aspects of this ride (you can easily imagine how difficult it must have been to drive a team pulling a loaded wagon up or down this long, steep, rain-muddied road) and the spectacular old-growth forest you'll see along the way make the ride a truly memorable one. Huge thanks are due to the volunteers of Oregon Equestrian Trails who keep this trail cleared of downed timber and rebuild the trail when it washes out.

The Ride: From the east side of the horse camp, follow Road 024 downhill 0.75 mile to the route of the historic wagon road. In several places the wagon road has become impassable or obliterated, so single-track trails are used to connect the road sections that remain. Some of these single-track connectors traverse steep hillsides before rejoining the wider track of the wagon road. After you cross Road 2044 (about 4 miles from camp) you'll ride on what the forest service says is the most intact section of the original wagon road. There are several small creeks to cross along the route that offer opportunities to water your horses.

Ray on Moose and Connie on Diamond, marveling at the size of the trees along the wagon road heading west.

A horse is dangerous at both ends and uncomfortable in the middle.

Ian Fleming
(author of the James Bond novels)

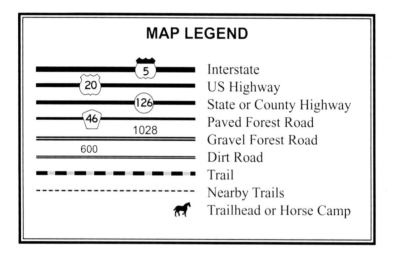

Silver Falls State Park

Howard Creek Horse Camp

Silver Falls is Oregon's largest state park, covering over 8,700 acres. It offers more than 20 miles of horse trails, a wonderful horse camp, and a day-use area with hitching rails, picnic table, fire pit, toilets, and enough parking for over a dozen trailers. The park is very popular with local riders, and it's easy to see why. The trails are wide and in excellent condition, the terrain is not difficult, and the forest is lush and varied. Reservations are required for the horse camp and it gets booked up early for summer weekends, so plan ahead. While you are there, be sure to take a hike to visit some of the park's spectacular waterfalls. (Sorry, horses aren't permitted on the waterfall trails so you'll have to do this on foot.)

In this chapter we describe four different loop trails in the park, but other loops are possible by connecting segments of the park's many trails.

South Falls

Howard Creek Horse Camp

Directions: Located about 21 miles east of Salem at Silver Falls State Park. From the junction of I-5 and Hwy. 22 (Mission St.) in Salem, go east on Hwy. 22 for 5.5 miles. Take exit 7 and continue east on Hwy. 214. After 15.5 miles, turn right into the park. Follow the signs to the horse camp, about 1 mile farther. The road is paved to the horse camp. The day-use parking area is just before you reach the horse camp. You can also do day rides from the 214 trailhead just south of the park entrance.

Elevation: 1,350 feet

Campsites: 5 sites with steel corrals for 4 horses each. One site is a pull-through and all others are back-in. All are level and graveled, with room for 2 vehicles. There is also a group site with corrals for 12 horses and parking for multiple vehicles.

Facilities: Portable toilets, manure bins. All sites have fire pits, picnic tables, and water spigots with potable water.

Permits: User fees for camping or for day use

Season: Year-round

Contact: 800-551-6949, www.oregonstateparks.org/park_211.php

The group campsite at Howard Creek horse camp.

Getting to Silver Falls State Park

Silver Falls Area Trails

Trail	Difficulty	Elevation	Round Trip
Buck Mountain Loop	Moderate	1,350-2,200	8 miles
Rackett-Perimeter Loop	Moderate	1,350-2,250	10 miles
Shellburg Falls	Moderate	1,350-2,350	14.5 miles
214/Smith Creek Loop	Moderate	1,350-2,000	7 miles

222 Silver Falls State Park / Howard Creek Horse Camp

Buck Mountain Loop

Trailhead: Start at Howard Creek Horse Camp or at the Howard Creek Trailhead day-use area
Length: 8 miles
Elevation: 1,350 to 2,200 feet
Difficulty: Moderate. Most of the trail is easy, but there may be some muddy sections on the western portion of the trail.
Season: Year-round, although the trail can be muddy and slick after a rain
Permits: Camping or day-use fee for state park
Facilities: Toilets, potable water, hitching rails, and manure bins at the horse camp and the day-use area. Stock water is available on the trail.

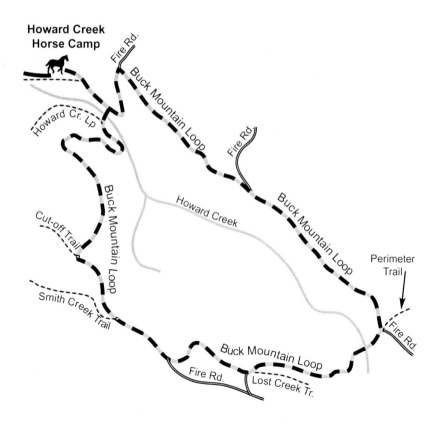

Highlights: This is a fun, easy ride, with nice wide trails through lovely forest terrain. Although you may encounter a few muddy spots on the west side of the loop, the trails are suitable for less-experienced riders and green horses. The trail is very well marked, with trail maps and/or trail markers posted at all junctions. Mileages are noted on all the trail maps.

The Ride: You can pick up the trail across from the entrance to the day-use area, or from the south side of campsite E in the horse camp. You will reach Buck Mountain Loop about 0.6 mile from the day-use area. We suggest going to the right so you take the loop counter-clockwise, as this puts the steepest section of the trail on the outbound, uphill leg. The trail crosses Howard Creek and climbs a ridge, intersecting with the Cut-off Trail in 1.5 miles. Continue to the left for another 0.5 mile and you'll pass the junction with the Smith Creek Trail. Stay to the left, and after another 0.9 mile, you'll reach a junction with a fire road and the Lost Creek Trail. Veer left and the trail will begin to descend. In 1.2 miles the Perimeter Trail will come in on the right. Again stay to the left and in 2.7 miles you'll reach the point where you entered the loop. Turn right to return to the horse camp or day-use area.

Debbie on Mel and Whitney on Dixie, checking out the detailed maps posted along the Silver Falls trails.

Rackett Ridge/Perimeter Loop

Trailhead: Start at Howard Creek Horse Camp or at the Howard Creek Trailhead day-use area
Length: 10 miles
Elevation: 1,350 to 2,250 feet
Difficulty: Moderate
Season: Year-round, although the trail can be muddy and slick after a rain
Permits: Camping or day-use fee for state park
Facilities: Toilets, potable water, hitching rails, and manure bins at the horse camp and the day-use area. Stock water is available on the trail.

Highlights: This trail is a little more challenging than the other trails in the park because of the steady climb to reach the top of Rackett Ridge. You'll gain 1,000 feet of elevation in 2 miles, so your horse will

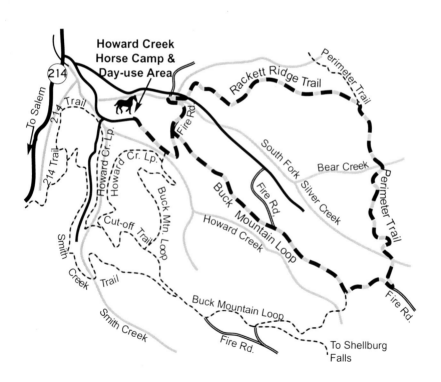

*Connie on Diamond and Lydia on Shadow,
enjoying the lush forest of the Perimeter Trail.*

be working. The Rackett Ridge Trail is wide and well maintained, while the Perimeter Trail is a single-track trail that makes a series of switchbacks down to Bear Creek and then up from the South Fork of Silver Creek to the Buck Mountain Trail. We encountered numerous holes in the Perimeter Trail where animal burrows had caved in, so be careful in this section.

The Ride: From the day-use area or the horse camp, head east to the Buck Mountain Loop and follow it to the left for 0.4 mile to a fire road that departs on your left. Take this road, and just after the bridge that crosses the South Fork of Silver Creek, pick up a single-track trail on the right between the creek and the paved road. The trail parallels the road for a short distance, then crosses it. You are now on the Rackett Ridge Trail. Continue about 2 miles to reach the Perimeter Trail. Horses are not permitted on the segment to the left, so turn right and follow it for 2.8 miles to the Buck Mountain Loop. Turn right and return on the eastern leg of the Buck Mountain Loop.

Shellburg Falls

Trailhead:	Start at Howard Creek Horse Camp or at the Howard Creek Trailhead day-use area
Length:	14.5 miles
Elevation:	1,350 to 2,350 feet
Difficulty:	Moderate. Most of the trail is easy, but there may be some muddy areas on the west section of the Buck Mountain trail.
Season:	Year-round, although the trail can be muddy and slick after a rain
Permits:	Camping or day-use fee for state park
Facilities:	Toilets, potable water, hitching rails, and manure bins at the horse camp and the day-use area. Stock water is available on the trail.

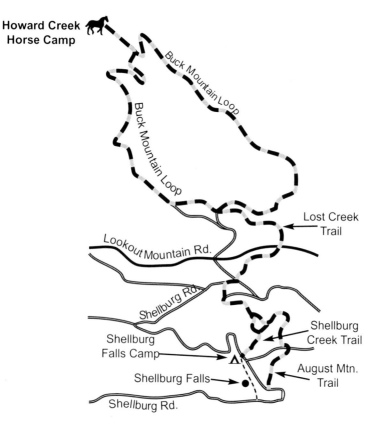

Silver Falls State Park / Howard Creek Horse Camp

Highlights: We were able to follow this beautiful trail only to Lookout Mountain road, for beyond that point the trails were temporarily closed for logging activity. There is a good trail to the Shellburg Falls area, and you can tie your horses at the Shellburg Falls Camp (horses aren't permitted on the Shellburg Falls Trail) and walk about 0.5 mile to the falls. The waterfall plunges 100 feet over a basalt outcropping. You can walk behind the falls.

The Ride: From the horse camp or day-use area, ride to the Buck Mountain Loop and follow it to the right. After 2.9 miles you'll reach the very pretty Lost Creek Trail. Veer right onto it (not onto the forest road) and follow it 0.9 mile to Lookout Mountain Road. Continue to Shellburg Road, veer left and follow it a short distance, then pick up the trail again on your left. In 0.6 mile you'll reach the Shellburg Creek Trail. Turn right and continue to Shellburg Road again. Veer left and it will lead you to Shellburg Falls Camp. Tie your horses here and continue on the footpath about 0.5 mile to the falls. To return, retrace your steps to the Buck Mountain Loop and turn right to complete a loop back to the horse camp.

Connie, Lydia, Debbie, and Whitney on the Lost Creek Trail on the way to Shellburg Falls.

214 Trail/Smith Creek Loop

Trailhead: Start at Howard Creek Horse Camp or at the Howard Creek Trailhead day-use area
Length: 7 miles
Elevation: 1,350 to 2,000 feet
Difficulty: Moderate. Most of the trail is easy, but there may be some muddy areas on the Buck Mountain trail.
Season: Year-round, although the trail can be muddy and slick after a rain
Permits: Camping or day-use fee for state park
Facilities: Toilets, potable water, hitching rails, and manure bins at the horse camp and the day-use area. Stock water is available on the trail.

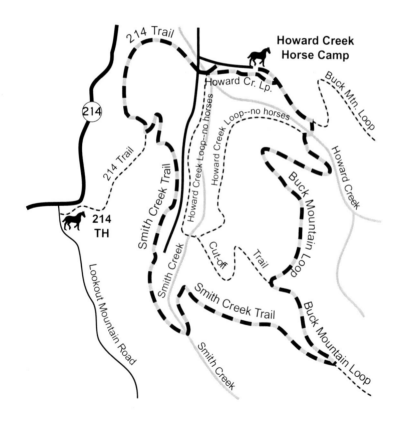

Debbie, Whitney, Lydia, and Connie moving out on the Smith Creek section of the loop.

Highlights: This is a nice ride that takes you west of the horse camp and then heads south parallel to Hwy. 214. It continues along the Smith Creek Trail and returns on the Buck Mountain Loop. Segments of the forest have been logged in the past, creating some variation in the types of vegetation you'll see along the way.

The Ride: From the horse camp or day use area, follow the road back toward the park entrance and in a short distance turn left onto the Howard Creek Loop. As soon as the trail crosses Howard Creek, veer right on the 214 Trail. This is an easy segment that is well suited to trotting, gaiting, or cantering. After a mile, turn left at the junction onto the Smith Creek Trail. Continue another 2.8 miles and turn left on the Buck Mountain Loop. Return to camp on the Buck Mountain Loop, staying to the right when the trail intersects with the Cut-off Trail and then the Howard Creek Loop. A short distance after crossing Howard Creek, veer left to return to the horse camp.

My experience of horses is that they never throw away a chance to go lame, and that in all respects they are well meaning and unreliable animals. I have also observed that if you refuse a high price for a favorite horse, he will go and lay down somewhere and die.

Mark Twain

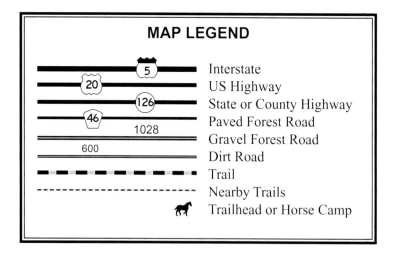

South Steens Campground

Frenchglen, Oregon

Steens Mountain is the largest fault block mountain in the Great Basin. When enormous pressure under the earth's crust pushed up one side of an existing fault line, it created the jagged east face of the Steens, which towers nearly a mile above the Alvord Desert below. The mountain slopes away more gradually to the west, but over time this side was carved by glaciers that created the Big Indian, Little Blitzen, Kiger, and Wildhorse gorges. Streams rush down these gorges today, creating lush vegetation around them. As you move away from the streams toward the canyon walls looming over 1,500 feet above, the grasses and cottonwoods give way to sagebrush and rabbitbrush, junipers, and stands of quaking aspen. Wildflowers are plentiful in season, and the area is home to wild horses, antelope, bighorn sheep, deer, and elk.

South Steens Campground lies near the entrances to the Big Indian and Little Blitzen gorges and provides access to the trails in this remarkable area.

*On the road to South Steens Campground.
The spectacular Little Blitzen Gorge is straight ahead.*

South Steens Campground

Directions: Approximately 90 miles south of Burns. Take Highway 20 through Burns and veer east on Highway 78. After 1.7 miles, turn right on Highway 205. Follow it 59 miles to the town of Frenchglen and continue another 10 miles. Turn left on the gravel South Loop Road (the sign mentions the Upper Blitzen River), drive 19 dusty and washboardy miles through spectacular scenery (watch for antelope and wild horses), and turn right into the campground.

Elevation: 5,300 feet

Campsites: 15 equestrian sites. There is also a family campground nearby. The corrals and hitching rails were built by Back Country Horsemen.

Facilities: Potable water, toilets, garbage cans, and manure bin. All sites have sturdy hitching rails, fire pits, and picnic tables. 5 sites have oversized corrals that can hold 2 horses. 6 sites are pull-throughs and the rest are back-ins. Several can accommodate 2 trailers.

Permits: Fee campground

Season: Summer through fall. (Fall has spectacular colors and fewer mosquitoes.)

Contact: Burns District Office, 541-573-4400, www.or.blm.gov/burns/recreation/camp.html

Jane enjoys the view over dinner at South Steens Campground.

Getting to South Steens

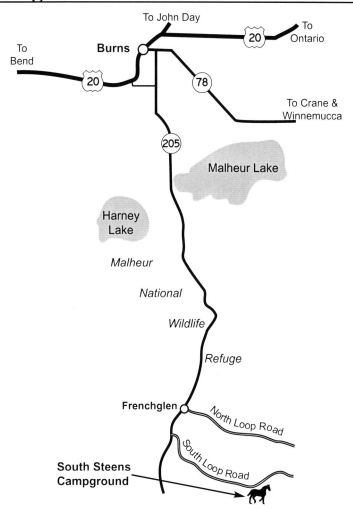

South Steens Area Trails

Trail	Difficulty	Elevation	Round Trip
Big Indian Trail	Moderate	5,300-7,000	18 miles
Little Blitzen Trail	Challenging	5,300-6,300	20 miles
Riddle Ranch	Easy	5,000-5,300	6 miles

Big Indian Trail

Trailhead:	Start at South Steens Campground
Length:	Maximum 18 miles round trip
Elevation:	5,300 to 7,000 feet
Difficulty:	Moderate: several water crossings
Season:	Summer through fall
Facilities:	Toilets and potable water at the campground. Stock water is available on the trail.

Highlights: Big Indian is the easier of the two canyon trails from South Steens Campground. The trail runs along the creek that flows through this U-shaped glaciated valley, as the canyon walls tower 1,000 feet overhead. Cottonwoods and tall grasses grow along the lovely Big Indian creek, and groves of quaking aspen provide intervals of welcome shade along the trail. Near the east end of the canyon, waterfalls cascade down the cliffs from all sides.

The Ride: Exit the horse camp using the single-track trail between campsites 9 and 10. The trail travels 2.3 miles over a rocky hillside before crossing Big Indian Creek and entering the canyon. Members of Back Country Horsemen of Oregon have painstakingly removed most of the rocks from the trail itself -- thank you, BCHO! Once in the

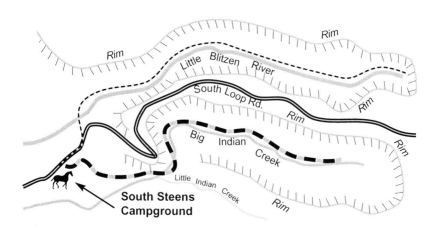

canyon, you'll marvel at the contrasts between the lush vegetation near the creek, the belt of dry sagebrush and rabbit brush along the base of the cliffs, and the jagged majesty of the cliffs themselves. In early summer, runoff from the melting snows above can create boggy areas in the trail. Mosquitoes can be thick in these areas. Wildflowers are spectacular in season. There is a lovely picnic spot in a grove of ancient cottonwoods along the grassy creek bank about 6.8 miles from the campground. Near the top of the canyon, the trail crosses just above a waterfall that you can hike down to on foot.

The first 2 miles of the trail cross a barren, rocky hillside that offers panoramic views to the west.

Then the trail follows Big Indian Creek beneath the cliffs of Big Indian Gorge.

Little Blitzen Trail

Trailhead: Start at South Steens Campground
Length: Maximum 20 miles round trip
Elevation: 5,300 to 6,300 feet
Difficulty: Challenging. In the first 2 miles inside the gorge there are several steep drop-offs along the narrow, rocky, and overgrown trail. After that, the valley widens and the going gets much easier.
Season: Summer through fall
Facilities: Toilets and potable water at the campground. Stock water is available on the trail.

Highlights: The trail parallels the Little Blitzen River as it runs through Little Blitzen Gorge. Sheer basalt cliffs tower more than 1,000 feet over the floor of this glaciated valley, and the many layers of lava that formed the cliffs are clearly visible. The lush grass, cottonwoods, and aspen near the river contrast sharply with the sagebrush steppe vegetation that blankets the slopes below the cliffs.

The Ride: Go through the gate to the left of the entrance to South Steens campground and turn right on South Loop Road. Follow the road 1.1 mile to the trailhead parking area, then continue on the road 0.2 mile farther to the trailhead itself. Turn left on the trail, which follows an arid hillside down to the first crossing of the Little Blitzen

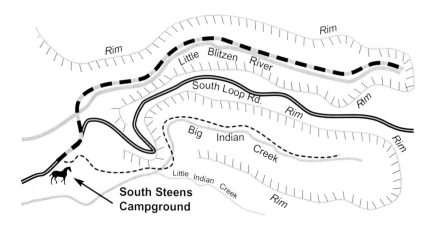

Julie and Perseus relax and enjoy the great views in Little Blitzen Gorge.

Whitney on Dixie, Deb on Mel, Lydia on Shadow, and Julie on Perseus, on the Little Blitzen Trail.

River, then up into the gorge. The next 2 miles of the trail are challenging: the trail is narrow, rocky, overgrown with brush, and in several spots it traverses hillsides that drop sharply to the rocky river bed below. After that, however, the gorge widens out and the going is much easier. There are several nice picnic spots along the creek or in the aspen groves where the horses can graze and you can lounge in the shade. The wildflowers are spectacular in early summer. The mosquitoes can be voracious, so make liberal use of mosquito repellent.

Riddle Ranch

Trailhead:	Start at South Steens Campground
Length:	6 miles round trip
Elevation:	5,000 to 5,300 feet
Difficulty:	Easy
Season:	Summer through fall
Facilities:	Toilets and potable water at the campground. Toilet at the Riddle Ranch. Stock water is available on the trail.

Highlights: In the early 1900s, bachelor brothers Walt, Fred, and Ben Riddle settled on the banks of the Little Blitzen River to raise cattle and horses. By taking control of the water in the area, they effectively made the nearby grazing areas unusable by anyone else. Today their ranch is owned and maintained by the BLM as a historic site. You can

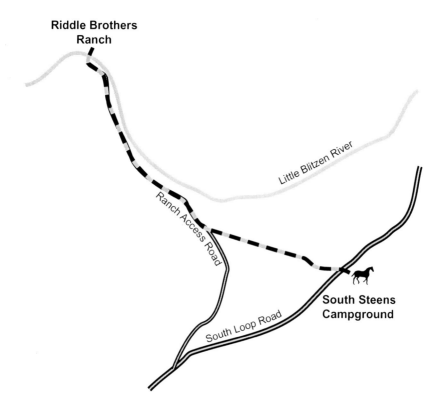

check out the barn, outbuildings, and farm implements, and can go inside Fred Riddle's cabin for a glimpse at how pioneer ranchers lived and worked. The ride to the ranch is on dirt roads that offer beautiful views of Steens Mountain.

The Ride: This is a short and easy arrival-day ride. Depart through the gate to the left of the campground entrance, cross the road, and follow the 1.4-mile single-track trail that leads to the ranch access road. Turn right and follow the access road 1.6 miles to the Riddle Ranch.

Pat on Zazu, Julie on Perseus, and Lydia on Shadow, on the road to the Riddle Ranch.

You can go inside Fred Riddle's historic ranch house.

If the world was truly a rational place, men would ride sidesaddle.

Rita Mae Brown

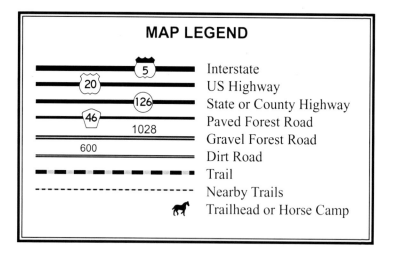

Sunrise Valley Ranch

Maury Mountains, Ochoco National Forest

Larry and Sue Fildes and two of their three grown children operate a guest facility on their working cattle ranch in the heart of the Maury Mountains. Located 65 miles east of Bend, the guest ranch serves 3 meals a day and provides guided horseback rides (on your horses only) in the beautiful country surrounding the ranch. There are few trails in the area and lots of fences to find gates through, so it's important to have a guide who can show you the way to the amazing geological features, ancient Indian artifacts, and historic pioneer homesteads that can be found in these forested hills. There are at least 14 different rides that you could do from the ranch, and Larry and Sue select which ones to take you on based on the interests and skills of the riders. The accommodations (for both horses and humans) are very nice, and the food is outstanding. Don't miss it!

Sunrise Valley Ranch guests gather to enjoy meals in the log-paneled guest house common room.

Sunrise Valley Ranch

Directions: Located 65 miles east of Bend. From Bend, drive east on Highway 20 about 43 miles to the town of Brothers. Turn left on Camp Creek Rd. (sign says Pringle Flat/Camp Creek/Dry Lake). In 7 miles there is a 4-way intersection where all the roads turn to gravel. Continue straight (slight jog to left) and continue 7 miles to a "T" intersection. Turn right on Camp Creek Rd. and drive 7 miles, then turn left on Tackman Rd. Watch the mileage carefully, as the Tackman Rd. turn is easy to miss. Follow Tackman Rd. 1.75 miles to Sunrise Valley Ranch.

Elevation: 4,350 feet

Campsites: The ranch accommodates 8 guests at a time, in a modern 4-bedroom, 2-bath bunkhouse that features a wide, shady veranda that looks out at the Maury Mountains.

Facilities: Full bed and board provided for guests and their horses: 3 hearty meals a day plus snacks for guests, hot showers, sturdy camp cots, and flush toilets. Corrals for 8 horses, with water and grass hay or alfalfa provided. Guests come for 3-5 days of guided rides, with all 5-day stays starting on Sunday and 3-day stays starting on Sunday, Monday, or Tuesday.

Permits: None. Fees for overnight lodging & boarding.

Season: June 1 through September 30

Contact: 541-477-3711 or sunrisevalleyranch@hotmail.com

Preparing to ride at the corrals. As usual, the guys are ready first.

Getting to Sunrise Valley Ranch

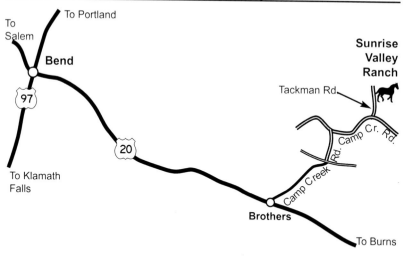

Sunrise Valley rides are ranch rides, not nose-to-tail rides on single-track trails.

A Sample of Sunrise Valley Trails

Trail	Difficulty	Elevation	Round Trip
Double Cabin Loop	Moderate	4,350-5,250	10 miles
Ranch Loop	Moderate	4,350-4,800	8.5 miles
Volcano Spg./Logan Butte	Moderate	4,125-4,375	13 miles

Double Cabin Loop

Trailhead: Start at Sunrise Valley Ranch
Length: 10 miles round trip
Elevation: 4,350 to 5,250 feet
Difficulty: Moderate
Season: June - September
Permits: None
Facilities: Full facilities at the ranch. Stock water is available on the trail.

Highlights: This ride departs from the entrance to the ranch and turns right on Tackman Road. After 0.5 mile a trail goes off to the left. Follow it 0.3 mile, cross Indian Creek, and continue along the bank of Double Cabin Creek. This portion of the trail is in beautiful Ponderosa forest, and in 1.4 miles it reaches the pretty Double Cabin Pond, a good

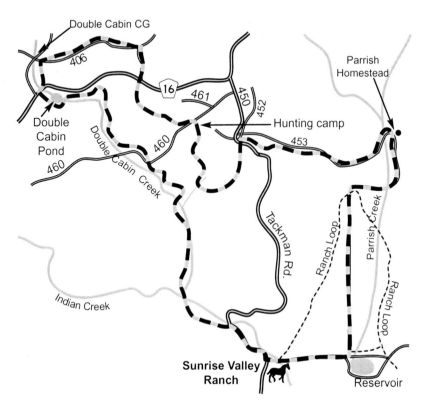

fishing spot. The trail then loops up and parallels Road 406, dropping down to a primitive hunting camp about 5.9 miles from the ranch. The Fildes' daughter, Becky, brought us a delicious picnic lunch at the camp. After lunch, we left the Ponderosa forest and headed across several arid juniper- and sage-covered ridges that provide views of Parrish Rim. At the base of Parrish Rim (7.25 miles from the ranch), we reached the old Parrish family homestead. You can still see the rose garden and apple orchard, a row of poplar trees, and the remains of the root cellar and the barn. The house fell down a few years ago so all that remains of it is a pile of debris. After this glimpse into the area's past, we headed back to the ranch.

Our group enjoys the picnic lunch cooked and delivered to us by the Fildes' daughter, Becky (to the right of the picnic table.)

Nancy on Aboo, Von on Pedro, and Chuck on Foxy, checking out the remains of the historic Parrish homestead.

Ranch Loop

Trailhead: Start at Sunrise Valley Ranch
Length: 8.5 miles round trip
Elevation: 4,350 to 4,800 feet
Difficulty: Moderate
Season: June-September
Permits: None
Facilities: Full facilities at the ranch. Stock water is available on the trail.

Highlights: This ride is typically the first one you'll do when you visit Sunrise Valley Ranch. It provides a nice orientation to the area and gives Larry, Sue, and Matt a chance to size up the capabilities and interests of the guests and their horses. If some of the guests want to do short rides and the others want something longer or more strenuous, they'll split the group up to accommodate you. As a result, this ride may vary a bit depending on the preferences and skill levels of the guests in residence that week.

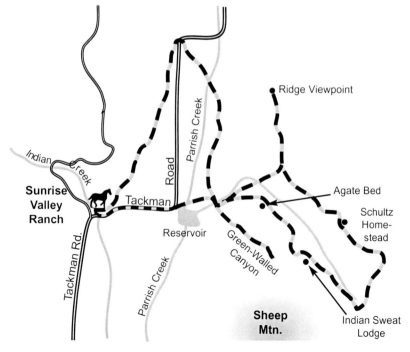

Matt on Cruiser, Von on Pedro, Nancy on Aboo, Whitney on Dixie, and Leo on Junior, heading down a draw on the ranch tour ride.

The variety of terrain you'll travel through is remarkable. You'll ride in the shadows of Sheep Mountain and Parrish Rim, take in the vistas from the tops of juniper-covered ridges, ride through deep gullies carved by seasonal creeks, travel through lush spring-fed meadows, and see Indian artifacts and relics from pioneer homesteads along the way.

Here's what our ride was like: about 0.7 mile east of the ranch we passed a reservoir that is home to a large beaver family. A mile or so later we came to an area that is one of only 2 places in the state where you can find snake agate, an rock with a scaly outer layer that covers creamy agate inside. Not far beyond we saw the remains of an Indian sweat lodge. About a mile farther we came upon the pioneer Schultz homestead--all that's left is a pile of planks and some fencing but it's easy to imagine what the old place must have been like. Four miles from the ranch we climbed a ridge to view the valleys below, then made our way back down and headed up a deep box canyon. The canyon was carved by a seasonal spring that has eroded the softer soils to reveal a layer of startlingly green rock. After that we traveled north through lush green meadows where cattle were happily grazing, then turned south and headed back to the ranch. For its variety and many interesting sights, this ride is hard to beat.

Volcano Spring/Logan Butte Loop

Trailhead: Start at Sunrise Valley Ranch
Length: 13 miles round trip
Elevation: 4,125 to 4,375 feet
Difficulty: Moderate
Season: June - September
Permits: None
Facilities: Full facilities at the ranch. Stock water is available on the trail.

Highlights: This ride took us to the fascinating Volcano Spring, where bentonite-laden water bubbles out of the ground. The spring has built a 4-foot high mound where the center appears to be solid ground but is really quicksand that's at least 8 feet deep. Then after a huge picnic lunch we traveled to the base of Logan Butte where the eroded soils and weird formations look like something straight out of a Yel-

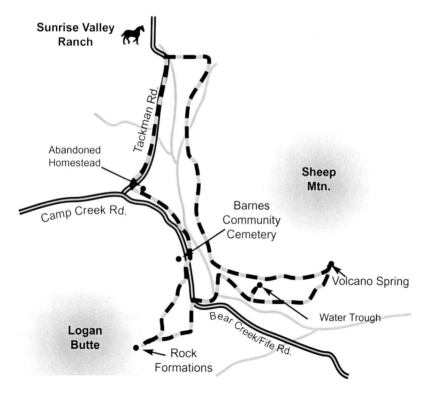

Nancy on Aboo and Whitney on Dixie, taking a look at the unusual geologic formations on Logan Butte.

lowstone Park geyser basin. If you search, you can find fossilized bone fragments here. Then we rode to the historic Barnes Community Cemetery, where you can see the 8 early settler's graves. The oldest is a Mr. Litton, who died in 1890. After that we headed back to the ranch. When you reach Tackman Road, you'll pass a weathered, deserted old homestead that provides yet another glimpse into the lives of the hardy folk who settled this remarkable country.

The abandoned homestead on Tackman Road.

When the horse's jaws are in motion, his mind is at rest.

Pete Rose

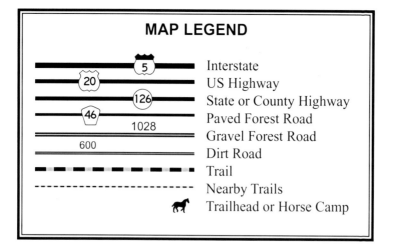

Triangle Lake Horse Camp

Mt. Hood National Forest

Triangle Lake Horse Camp is located in the Cascades between Mt. Hood and Mt. Jefferson and is an easy drive from Portland, Salem, or Bend. The horse camp provides access to the Olallie Scenic Area, the Pacific Crest Trail, and the Mt. Jefferson Wilderness Area. Olallie Scenic Area has numerous trails and over 30 lakes to explore, although most are a bit of a distance from the horse camp. Few of the trails are well signed, so it's best to pick up an area map from the Olallie Lake Resort store. The horse camp itself is well laid out, with screening vegetation separating the campsites. The Pacific Crest Trail is only a short distance from camp, running north into the Warm Springs Reservation and south through Olallie Scenic Area and beyond.

Triangle Lake lies at the base of Olallie Butte.

Triangle Lake Horse Camp

Directions: Located 57 miles southeast of Estacada and 33 miles northeast of Detroit. *From Estacada*, drive southeast on Hwy. 224 for 25 miles, turn right on Road 46 and continue 22 miles. Go left on Road 4690 for 8 miles, then right on Road 4220 and continue 2 miles to Triangle Horse Camp. *From Detroit*, head northeast on Road 46 and drive 23 miles. Turn right on Road 4690 and continue 8 miles, then turn right on Road 4220 and drive 2 miles to the camp.

Elevation: 4,550 feet

Campsites: 8 sites with log corrals for 4 horses each. All sites are back-in and fairly level, and some are large enough for two vehicles.

Facilities: Toilet, stock water, no drinking water. Handicapped access mounting ramp.

Permits: User fee for camp.

Season: Summer through fall

Contact: Clackamas Ranger District, 503-630-6861, www.fs.fed.us/r6/mthood/recreation/campgrounds/index.html

Shadow is hanging out in the Triangle Lake corrals.

Getting to Triangle Lake Horse Camp

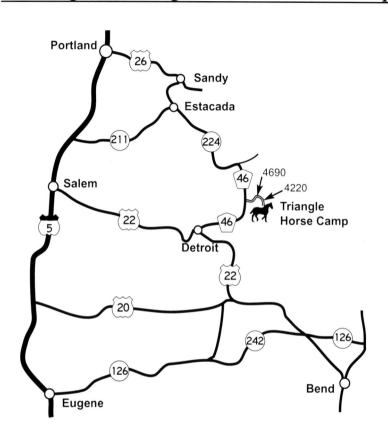

Triangle Lake Area Trails

Trail	Difficulty	Elevation	Round Trip
Jefferson Park	Difficult	5,300-6,900	14 miles
Lodgepole Trail	Challenging	4,400-5,100	varies
Pacific Crest Trail North	Moderate	4,400-5,000	varies
Pacific Crest Trail South	Moderate	4,600-5,400	varies
Russ Lake Loop	Easy	4,500-4,650	3 miles

Jefferson Park

Trailhead: Start at Olallie Lake Resort (extremely limited parking on the side of the road) or at Horseshoe Lake campground (narrow, rutted access road)
Length: 22 miles round trip from Olallie Resort, or 14 miles round trip from Horseshoe Lake campground
Elevation: 5,300 to 6,900 feet
Difficulty: Difficult: steep and extremely rocky in places
Season: Summer through fall
Permits: User fee for horse camp
Facilities: Toilets at Olallie Lake Resort or Horseshoe Lake campground. Stock water is available on the trail.

Highlights: Jefferson Park is a beautiful destination, so we were delighted to read on the Olallie Resorts website that Jefferson Park is one of the area's featured horse trails. However, we do not recommend it.

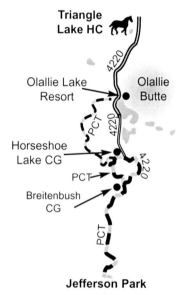

Triangle Lake Horse Camp

Whitney leads Dixie across a rather nasty rockslide.

For starters, if you trailer your horse as close to Mt. Jefferson as you can get, you'll drive a heavily-traveled, rocky, bone-jarring one-lane road for over an hour (repeatedly trying to find spots to pull over so oncoming vehicles can pass), and once you begin you can't change your mind -- you must go all the way to Horseshoe Lake campground before there is room to turn your trailer around. The road is not maintained beyond Horseshoe Lake. For another thing, this is a pretty strenuous trail, especially the last 3 miles before Jefferson Park, when you'll gain and then lose 1,500 feet of elevation, only to turn around and repeat the effort on your return trip. And for a third thing, some segments are on loose rock that can be difficult for horses to manage. Snowfields are also a factor, even in late August. There are better and easier ways to reach the lovely Jefferson Park, so we don't recommend this ride.

The Ride: From Horseshoe Lake campground, you can ride along the extremely rocky and rutted Road 4220 for 2.5 miles or take a tie trail to the PCT. We took the road because it is about the same distance but isn't as steep as the PCT route. Just past Breitenbush campground, pick up the PCT where it crosses Road 4220 and follow it 4.4 miles to the beautiful Jefferson Park.

Lodgepole Trail

Trailhead: Start at Triangle Lake Horse Camp
Length: 5.6 miles round trip to Lower Lake, 8 miles round trip to Fork Lake, or 11.2 miles round trip to Red Lake. Or you can do a 10-mile loop by going to Fork Lake and returning to camp on the PCT
Elevation: 4,400 to 5,100 feet
Difficulty: Challenging: very rocky and rutted, with fairly steep climbs and descents over ridges. There are a few places where the trail almost disappears in grassy meadows.
Season: Summer through fall
Permits: User fee for the horse camp
Facilities: Toilet and stock water at the horse camp. No water on the trail.

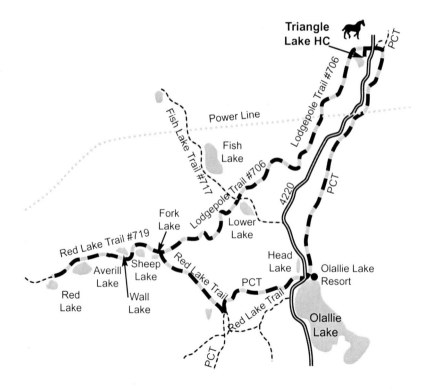

Triangle Lake Horse Camp

Highlights: This is a pretty forested trail, but is quite rocky and has some sections that climb steeply and then descend just as steeply as the trail crosses several ridges. Most of the trail is heavily forested, with several nice lakes along the way. There are a few places where the trail nearly disappears in the thick grasses of sunny meadows. Note that horses are not permitted to drink from the lakes because of the bank damage and water turbidity they can cause.

The Ride: Just north of campsite #1 and almost across from the camp's notice board, pick up the trail out of the horse camp. A short distance from camp you'll come to an unmarked junction with the Lodgepole Trail. Turn left and about 2.8 miles from camp you'll reach Lower Lake. If you continue the entire 5.6 miles to Red Lake you will pass Sheep Lake, Wall Lake, and Averill Lake on the way. If you want to make it into a loop ride, turn left onto the Red Lake Trail at Fork Lake, follow it 1 mile to the PCT, and turn left to take the PCT back to the horse camp.

*Whitney on Dixie, on the Lodgepole Trail
not far from Triangle Lake horse camp.*

Pacific Crest Trail North

Trailhead: Start at Triangle Lake Horse Camp
Length: 12 miles round trip to Lemiti Meadows
Elevation: 4,400 to 5,000 feet
Difficulty: Moderate
Season: Summer through fall
Permits: User fee for the horse camp
Facilities: Toilet and stock water at the horse camp. Stock water is available on the trail.

Highlights: We weren't able to travel very far north on the PCT because of bridge construction work that was being done over the south

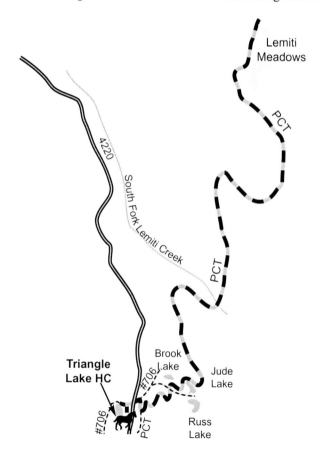

fork of Lemiti Creek. However, the bridge work is now complete and the trail is beautifully maintained by the Oregon Muleskinners for some distance. The PCT north of Triangle Lake is on the Warm Springs Indian Reservation.

The Ride: Just north of campsite #1 and almost across from the camp's notice board, pick up the trail out of the horse camp. A short distance from camp you'll come to an unmarked junction with the Lodgepole Trail #706. Turn right, and in about 0.1 mile you'll cross Road 4220. 0.2 mile after that you'll veer right on the PCT access trail, and 0.1 mile later you'll reach the PCT. Turn left. In another 0.4 mile you'll cross the Russ Lake Trail. Continue on the PCT and in another 0.2 mile you'll pass Jude Lake. The PCT climbs for the next 1.75 miles or so, then levels out for several miles before descending to Lemiti Meadow. Return to camp by retracing your steps.

Lydia and Shadow take a breather on a rainy day along the PCT north of Triangle Lake.

Pacific Crest Trail South

Trailhead: Start at Triangle Lake Horse Camp
Length: 6.7 miles round trip to Olallie Lake; 10.4 miles round trip to Cigar Lake
Elevation: 4,600 to 5,000 feet to Olallie Lake; 4,600 to 5,400 to Cigar Lake
Difficulty: Moderate
Season: Summer through fall
Permits: User fee for the horse camp
Facilities: Toilet and stock water at the horse camp. No water on the trail.

Highlights: After riding the rocky Lodgepole Trail, riding the PCT is an absolute joy. This section of the trail is beautifully maintained by the Muleskinners of Oregon and is nearly rock-free. You can trot or

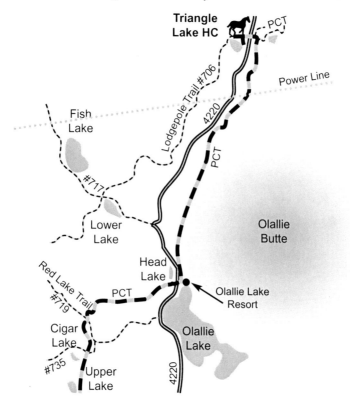

Lydia on Shadow and Whitney on Dixie, gaiting on the PCT just north of Olallie Lake Resort.

gait easily here. The trail is forested as it runs along the base of Olallie Butte. When you reach Olallie Lake you can stop in at the resort store and enjoy the spectacular view of Mt. Jefferson over Olallie Lake while you sip a cold soft drink. The PCT continues south, of course, past Cigar Lake and Upper Lake and beyond. It is much rockier and not as well maintained south of Olallie Lake Resort.

The Ride: Just north of campsite #1 and almost across from the camp's notice board, pick up the trail out of the horse camp. A short distance from camp you'll come to an unmarked junction with the Lodgepole Trail. Turn right and in about 0.1 mile you'll cross Road 4220, 0.2 mile after that you'll veer right on the PCT access trail, and 0.1 mile later you'll reach the PCT. Turn right. The trail travels along the lower flank of Olallie Butte until it reaches Olallie Lake Resort. Then the trail re-crosses Road 4220 and veers west. After 1.4 miles, the Red Lake Trail #719 crosses the PCT. Go straight, and in 0.65 mile you'll reach Cigar Lake and trail #735, which goes right to Double Peaks and left to the Red Lake Trail. If you stay left and continue another 0.35 mile you'll reach Upper Lake.

Russ Lake Loop

Trailhead: Start at Triangle Lake Horse Camp
Length: 3.2 miles round trip
Elevation: 4,500 to 4,650 feet
Difficulty: Easy
Season: Summer through fall
Permits: User fee for horse camp
Facilities: Toilet and stock water at the horse camp. No water is available on the trail.

Highlights: This is a short ride that visits three little lakes near Triangle Lake horse camp. It's a nice warm-up ride when you first arrive or a take-it-easy ride the day after doing one of the area's more strenuous trails. This loop travels through pretty forested terrain and past the lakes. Note that horses are not permitted to drink at any of the

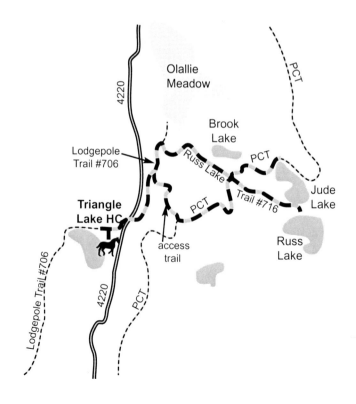

Mist rises from the surface of Jude Lake on a cool, rainy morning.

lakes in the Olallie Scenic Area because of the bank erosion and water turbidity that they can cause.

The Ride: Just north of campsite #1 and almost across from the camp's notice board, pick up the trail out of the horse camp. A short distance from camp you'll come to an unmarked junction with the Lodgepole Trail. Turn right and in about 0.1 mile you'll cross Road 4220. Continue another 0.2 mile to the junction with the PCT access trail; veer left to stay on the Lodgepole Trail, and in another 0.2 mile you'll reach the junction with the Russ Lake Trail. Turn right and ride 0.2 mile to pass Brook Lake and continue 0.1 mile to the junction with the PCT. Turn left on the PCT and go 0.2 mile to reach the north shore of Jude Lake. Retrace your steps and this time turn left toward Russ Lake. The Russ Lake trail ends at Russ Lake. Return to the PCT and turn left. In 0.3 mile you'll reach the horse camp access trail, which will carry you back to the camp.

Horses leave hoofprints on your heart.

Anonymous

MAP LEGEND

═══5═══	Interstate
══20══	US Highway
──126──	State or County Highway
──46──	Paved Forest Road
──1028──	Gravel Forest Road
──600──	Dirt Road
■ ■ ■ ■	Trail
- - - - -	Nearby Trails
🐎	Trailhead or Horse Camp

Tryon Creek State Park

Portland, Oregon

Tryon Creek State Park is a wonderful place to ride in the winter because the well-gravelled paths provide good footing even in wet weather. It's also nice riding on a hot summer day, when the dense tree canopy provides an oasis of shade. There are 5 miles of equestrian trails in the park, which may not seem like a lot. But considering that the park is only 6 miles from downtown Portland, it's almost a miracle that there are any horse trails there at all. Tryon Creek runs through the middle of the park, and both of the park's horse trail loops run down to the creek and back up again.

Tryon Creek State Park's year-round bridle paths beckon.

Tryon Creek State Park

Directions: 6 miles south of downtown Portland. If you are coming *from the north*, drive south on I-5 and take exit 297 toward Terwilliger Blvd. Merge onto SW Barbur Blvd., and in 0.1 mile turn right on SW Terwilliger Blvd. Go 1.6 miles and at the traffic circle take the second exit and stay on Terwilliger Blvd. The park is 0.8 mile ahead on the right. If you are coming *from the south*, take exit 297 (Terwilliger Blvd.). Turn right on Terwilliger and go 1.5 miles, then at the traffic circle take the second exit and stay on Terwilliger Blvd. The park is 0.8 mile ahead on the right.

Elevation: 275 feet

Campsites: Camping is not permitted in Tryon Creek State Park

Facilities: Toilet, stock water, hitching posts, handicapped-access loading ramp. If hikers' cars haven't filled up the equestrian parking area, there is room for 4 or 5 trailers. If you are planning to bring 3 or more trailers to the park, call 503-636-9886 ext. 222 to make arrangements.

Permits: None

Season: Year round

Contact: www.oregonstateparks.org/park_144.php, or 503-636-9886

Tryon's equestrian parking area is fairly large, but trailer parking may be limited by cars overflowing from the hikers' lot.

Getting to Tryon Creek State Park

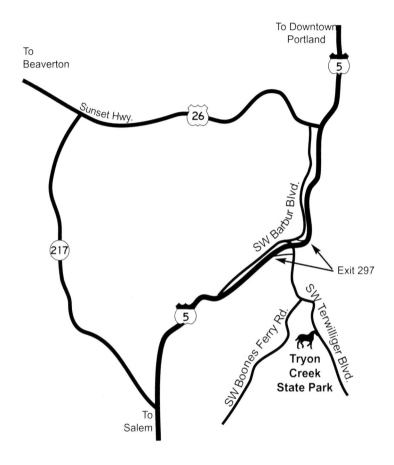

Tryon Creek State Park Trails

Trail	Difficulty	Elevation	One way
Boones Ferry Trail	Easy	215-270	0.4 mile
Englewood Trail	Easy	250-350	0.5 mile
North Horse Loop	Easy	120-325	2.1 miles
West Horse Loop	Easy	110-290	3.1 miles

Tryon Creek Trails

Trailhead: Start at the equestrian trailhead at Tryon Creek State Park
Length: 5 miles of horse trails, with several possible loop rides
Elevation: 110 to 350 feet
Difficulty: Easy
Season: Year round
Permits: None
Facilities: Toilet, stock water, hitching posts, handicapped-access loading ramp, parking for 4-5 trailers

Highlights: Tryon Creek's horse trails aren't long, but they are good ones, especially considering the park's urban location. The horse trail network consists of two loop trails and a couple of short side trails. There is a moderate amount of elevation gain/loss on the trails, so while the ride is short your pony will get a bit of a workout. Remember that we share these trails with hikers and dog walkers, and they

Tex gazes down the Englewood Trail on a sunny day.

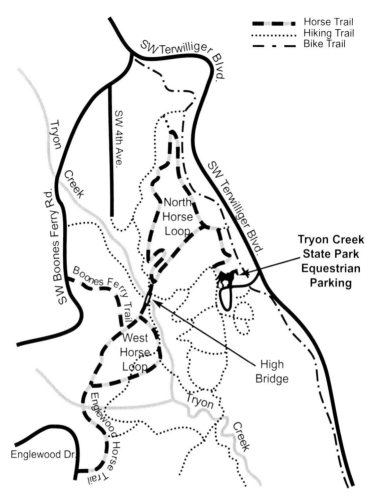

vastly outnumber equestrian users and are probably not familiar with horses.

The Ride: To create the longest possible trail, ride one side of the North Horse Loop, cross the High Bridge, ride the entire West Horse Loop with detours on the out-and-back Boones Ferry and Englewood trails, re-cross the High Bridge, and return to the trailhead via the other side of the North Horse Loop. The park is in the deep ravine carved by Tryon Creek, so you'll lose and then gain about 200 feet of elevation twice during the ride. The footing is great, even in wet weather, so your biggest hazard will be the people, dogs, and strollers you share the trail with.

Tryon Creek Trails (cont.)

The High Bridge crosses Tryon Creek and links the North and West Horse Trails.

Tex enjoys the tall trees and dense shade on a warm summer day.

Tryon Creek State Park 271

Jane appreciates the park's good footing on a drizzly day in winter.

Helpful maps and signs along the trail tell you where you are and what's around the bend.

May the horse be with you.

Anonymous

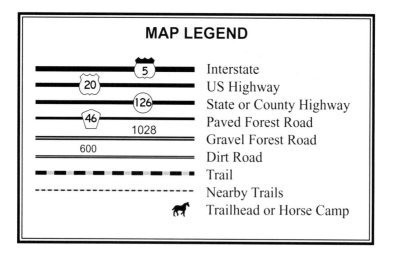

Willamette Mission State Park

Salem, Oregon

Willamette Mission State Park is the site of the historic Jason Lee mission, the first Methodist mission in Oregon. While Lee wasn't very successful in converting Indians to Christianity, his mission provided stability and leadership to white settlers. Lee founded Willamette University and played an important political role in making Oregon part of the United States.

The park features 7 miles of level, easy horse trails that go through forests and meadows, past working farmland, and along the bank of the Willamette River and Windsor Island Slough. The park also has the only overnight horse-camping facilities in the Willamette Valley. It provides a nice base camp for exploring the park and other day-riding areas in the Willamette Valley. And it's a great spot for an after-work ride or a leisurely weekend ride.

The trail runs along the bank of the Willamette River.

Willamette Mission Horse Camp

Directions: Located 7 miles north of Salem and 35 miles south of Portland. From I-5, take exit 263 (Brooks/Gervais exit) and turn west on Brooklake Road. Drive 1.75 miles and turn right on Wheatland Road. The park is 2.4 miles ahead on the left.

Elevation: 110 feet

Campsites: 4 sites with log corrals for 4 horses each. All sites are large enough for two vehicles, and 2 sites are pull-throughs.

Facilities: Toilet, drinking water, manure bin, garbage cans. Day-use area has a toilet and parking for 100+ trailers.

Permits: User fees for day use or for camping. Reservations required for the horse camp. Call 800-452-5687 for reservations.

Season: The horse camp is open May-October. The day-use area is year round, but some trails may be closed in winter. Call 503-393-1172 for winter closure information.

Contact: www.oregonstateparks.org/park_139.php or 503-551-6949

The corrals at Willamette Mission are sturdy and the campsites are grass covered and widely spaced.

Willamette Mission State Park

Getting to Willamette Mission

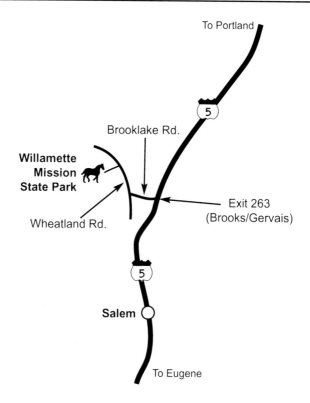

Willamette Mission Trails

Trail	Difficulty	Elevation	Round Trip
Willamette Mission	Easy	90-125	varies

Willamette Mission Trails

Trailhead: Start at the day-use parking area at Willamette Mission State Park

Length: 7 miles of horse trails. Several loops are possible.

Elevation: 90 to 125 feet

Difficulty: Easy

Season: Year round, but some trails may be closed because of seasonal flooding. Call 503-393-1172 for winter closure information.

Permits: Day-use fee

Facilities: Toilets, drinking water, reservation-only horse camp, tons of parking in day-use area. Stock water is available on the trail.

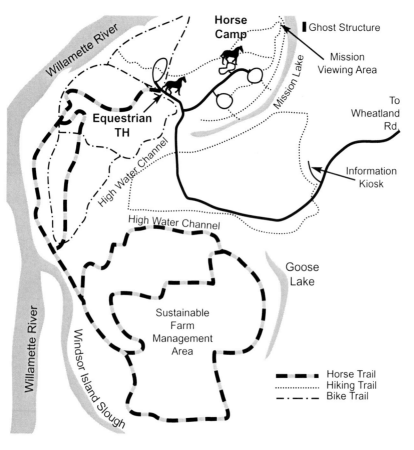

Willamette Mission State Park 277

Karen on Rudie and Cindy on Cairo cruising along the edge of the farmland at the south end of the park.

Highlights: The park's trails run through densely-forested areas, in open expanses of scotch broom and Oregon grape, around the edges of cultivated fields, along the shore of the Willamette River, and past Windsor Island Slough. There is a hitching rail near a pretty picnic spot on the bank of the Willamette. With the exception of some seasonal closures due to flooding, the trails are open year round. The footing in some spots can be muddy in winter.

The Ride: The trail departs from the southwestern edge of the parking area. It runs through a shady forested area, then enters an open meadow. Keep an eye out for osprey nests in the tops of trees. About 1.25 miles from the parking area you'll get a nice view of the Willamette River. This initial portion of the trail is popular with bicyclists and dog walkers. Then the trail runs south to Windsor Island Slough, where there's a spot to water your horse. From here the trails are used almost exclusively by equestrians, and you'll ride through more forest and around working farmland. Several alternative loops are possible.

Willamette Mission (continued)

Note: In late 2008 it was announced that as part of a Willamette River restoration project, a dike that has altered the flow of the river since the 1940s will be removed. This will allow the river to bend and flow through the area now known as Mission Lake, which will create more habitat for native species. It is not known how this change will affect the trail system, but park managers have indicated that equestrians will continue to have access to the park's trails. Public comment will be sought on the park's recreation plans, which were still being designed when this book went to press.

Willamette Mission has a huge parking area for equestrians.

Windsor Slough offers a place to water your horse along the trail.

Cindy on Cairo out in front, with Karen riding Rudie and leading ReaCo on an after-work ride.

Diane and Bucky enjoy the view of the Willamette River while on a winter ride on Diane's Tennessee Walkers.

Tribute to Luke

Thank you, dear friend, for all the fun we had together and all the lessons I learned from you, for your beautiful eyes that gazed at me and made my heart sing, for your wonderful rocking-horse canter that was so much fun to ride, for your nickering at me when I called your name, and for taking such good care of me when we were trail riding and horse camping together. I shall miss the adventures we had, but most of all I will miss you. My life has been so enriched by you.

So I say farewell to you, my Luke. We shall meet again in another time and place. So run free, go find your dear pasture mate, Caleb, who is waiting for you. Now your spirits can meet and become one again.

God bless you, my dear friend, and may your soul rest in peace.

Whitney Rhetts

Whitney and Luke cantering across Wickiup Plain.